View from
My Window

View from
My Window

Carol A. Klein

ISBN (Paperback): 979-8-9884037-6-0
ISBN (Hardcover): 979-8-9882956-2-4
ISBN (eBook): 979-8-9882956-1-7

Dedication

To my Heavenly Father…

Whose love, and light on my path, has guided me on the journey
of my earthly life, and will take me to my eternal life.

To my husband David…

For his commitment to us. For his encouragement, protection,
and guidance, which inspired me to take chances, stretch and
grow. For his integrity and faithfulness. For his obedience to God,
allowing him to care for me in ways I may not have deserved,
and didn't know I needed. Most of all, for his love through
which I am abundantly blessed!

To my children…

Who have broadened my perspective of life, challenged me to
be the best version of myself, and provided valuable learning
opportunities. Who have increased my capacity to love, forgive,
and appreciate our God given differences. My children, gifts from
God, priceless treasures, inexplicable joy!

A Time for All Events in Life

3 For everything there is an appointed time,
and an appropriate time for every activity on earth:
2 A time to be born, and a time to die;
a time to plant, and a time to uproot what was planted;
3 a time to kill, and a time to heal;
a time to break down, and a time to build up;
4 a time to weep, and a time to laugh;
a time to mourn, and a time to dance.
5 A time to throw away stones, and a time to gather stones;
a time to embrace, and a time to refrain from embracing;
6 a time to search, and a time to give something up as lost;
a time to keep, and a time to throw away;
7 a time to reep, and a time to sew;
a time to keep silent, and a time to speak.
8 A time to love, and a time to hate;
a time for war, and a time for peace.

Man Is Ignorant of God's Timing

9 What benefit can a worker gain from his toil?
10 I have observed the burden
that God has given to people to keep them occupied.
11 God has made everything fit beautifully in its appropriate time,
but he has also placed ignorance in the human heart
so that people cannot discover what God has ordained,
from the beginning to the end of their lives.

Enjoy Life in the Present

12 I have concluded that there is nothing better for people
than to be happy and to enjoy
themselves as long as they live,
13 and also that everyone should eat and drink,
and find enjoyment in all his toil,
for these things are a gift from God.

God's Sovereignty

14 I also know that whatever God does will endure forever;
nothing can be added to it, and nothing taken away from it.
God has made it this way, so that men will fear him.
15 Whatever exists now has already been, and whatever
will be has already been;
for God will seek to do again what has occurred in the past.

Ecclesiastes 3:1–15, NET

Forward

I grew up in a two-story home. My ten by twelve bedroom with a closet was at the top of the stairway to the right, the southeast corner with one window facing east, and one south.

I watched the world from those two windows. The sun rising, shadows of the sunset. Clouds changing shapes as they passed over my small place in the world, headed for destinations unknown. The moon and twinkling stars lighting up the night, and other times only the street lights broke the darkness. I could see the wind blow through the trees, see the lightning, hear the thunder, and watch snowflakes fall. Familiar cars would drive past on the way to their destination, bicyclist peddled on their way, and people out for a walk. Birds would sing, coming and leaving with the seasons. These though were not the limitations to the view from my window.

My imagination carried me to many places. I met so many people and talked to them about their lives. Sometimes it was just quietly sitting and absorbing the beauty around me. Many were my conversations with God about that which was currently on my mind and happening in my life. I would hum or just softly sing a favorite song. My imagination shaping my dreams, designing my goals, expressing my heart, and acquainting me with the person God created me to be.

Much of my life has been impacted by my perspective in the many moments which I have lived. It has served to develop character, ambitions, and passion, giving birth to creativity and possibilities. Weeding through my dreams and goals, nurturing some, leaving others behind.

In the *View from My Window*, I take you on a journey through moments in my life, each one playing a role in bringing me to the place I am in today, the person God created me to be. I am confident that the work is not done, the journey is not over, and the moments have not ended. As God has always promised in Jeremiah 29:11 (TLB), "For I know the plans I have for you, says the Lord. They are plans for good and not for evil, to give you a future and a hope."

May you find blessings and inspiration for your own life out of the abundance of God's great love, mercy, and grace.

For from his fullness Carol has received, grace upon grace. (John 1:16, ESV)

Contents

CHAPTER 1

The Season of Retirement

Perspective: the season of retirement. Like every phase of life, there is no one specific manual to help you navigate the practical everyday changes and routines. It makes sense. No two of us are alike, not even the husband and wife of many years, experiencing the same thing for the first time. Clinging to my anchor of hope for the future through Jesus, I move forward into the inevitable tomorrows until they are no more.

Now, that might sound a bit depressing, but not if you are moving forward with the knowledge that where you are going, God has already been there, and through Jesus, He is eager to walk the path ahead with you.

Two weeks into the long-awaited, much-anticipated, exciting event of retirement, I find myself pondering, no, more like analyzing, down to the minutest degree, my feelings, expectations, purpose, hopes, dreams, and details of where I am and what is next. In these few days, many questions I have not yet confronted have surfaced, but the time has come for confrontation.

Being a practical, organized, in charge, manager-of-all-things (well, sort of) person, I resort to that which is familiar and proven successful—journaling. Getting it out of my head onto a paper where I can stare it down has always helped to bring clarity to a situation.

In the moment, it feels like a jumbled mess, a ball of tangled Christmas lights in dire need of careful sorting. Monumental as the task may appear, it's not going to win. I am tenacious with an iron grip and a focused mindset. This isn't the first bull I have taken by the horns and wrestled to the ground, and Lord willing, it won't be the last. Let the fun begin!

My anchor of hope…what exactly do I mean?

There is no lack of self-help books, videos, conferences, blogs, studies, groups, and advice givers out there for you to invest your time and money into, each promising to be just what you need, when you need it, providing answers. Just follow their easy five-step program to success.

Don't get me wrong, this is not (well, not completely) sarcasm on my part. I have tried some, with a degree of success and failure, but none have yielded the result that my heart and soul were searching for. Let us be practical, no one has that much time, money, or resources to invest.

What exactly is my "only anchor"? The answer will interest some, turn others completely off, and clearly relate to those sharing the same anchor. It is simply the teachings of Jesus in God's Word to us—the Bible.

I started into this relationship with Jesus at the young age of four, and have, throughout my life, depended on the guidance I have received through a daily walk of faith. Though not a book with specific chapter titles for each stage and situation in life, the Bible is an all-inclusive book that provides answers to the challenges faced in those stages and situations. Now, in the first weeks of retirement, my expectations remain unchanged and steadfast.

Look to the Bible, and see what God has to say, and bathe everything in prayer.

Before answers, there have to be questions. Before directions is the opportunity of paths. Moving forward requires knowing from whence you have come and where you are at, a willingness to be stretched and grown, and an eagerness to embrace the unknown.

Many people enter into retirement with a plan. If you had ever asked me where I thought, or would like, to be in five years, my answer would always be, "Wherever God wants me." Clearly not a planner, and retirement is no different. I have but one plan: to not get up at 4:30 am. This has been accomplished!

Two weeks into retirement, where exactly do I stand? To know this, I must first examine the ponderings and questions these two weeks have yielded.

CHAPTER 2

Lists

Perspective: lists. Always a good thing to have. If it accomplishes nothing else, at the end of the day, the number of things you manage to cross off gives you a sense of accomplishment, and we all need to feel accomplished. A list has the power to move you through the day, from morning rise to evening rest.

I love the sense of accomplishment. It gives purpose to my day and is proof that I have not just been wasting time! If I was taught anything growing up, it was that you do not waste time. There is always something that needs to be done, and idle hands are the devil's playground. We shall have none of that!

Not surprising that the first thing I did in retirement was to "make a list," contents of the same being the product of my expectations. Unfortunately, I have one rather large flaw when it comes to "making a list." It is always unreasonable, reflecting my expectations, far exceeding my ability to accomplish, and at the end of the day, instead of feeling accomplished, I feel inadequate. Oh, you can tell me that I did a great job, but I will insist that I should have done better. Crazy? Yes, and deep down, even I know that.

Now portions of my list have been developing for over forty years. Many things on the list were for that magical "someday" when I would have time. Well, that time has arrived! It is called "retirement," and I will attack that list with tornado force.

Somewhere in my mindset was a six-day deadline for accomplishment. Really? Well, ok, maybe six weeks, but that's final! Get the picture?

Why so driven?

Well, for over forty years, my life has been ruled by a time frame set by the clock, the boss, the task at hand, and the number of hours of daylight in a single day. More often than not, the deadlines were more perceived in my mind than enforced by an authority. Nonetheless, they were real to me. Accomplishment equaled integrity, dependability, and worthiness.

One day I was employed, and the next day I was not. Unexpected reality gave rise to unanticipated challenges. Permission to relax, without guilt, or relinquished responsibility does not equal unworthiness; unemployment is not the loss of intelligence, skills, and abilities; and free time is not defined as uselessness. Yet, I feel the need to prove myself worthy.

The answer—a list, and the accomplishment of the same equals "overcomer," "winner." Score: Carol, 1; bull, 0. Yeah, not so much. Two weeks, fifteen days, and crossed off the list…weeds have been pulled; a lot of weeds have been pulled. And you know what? They grow back! So here I have it, a new job in retirement with a lifetime of promised "job security." Thank you, Adam and Eve!

Seems as though it is time for a deeper, longer look into "The Anchor" better known as God's Word—the Bible. New questions are begging for answers: Why do I feel like an outsider? Why this sense of loss over something I chose to give up? Isolation, is it real or imagined? Life has a new rhythm; how do I learn it? I am not working for a paycheck; does that make me a slacker? My worthiness is in Christ Jesus, so why am I feeling unworthy? For years my husband has worked from home and handled many of the household chores, so what is my role? How does my invasion of his territory (which is really ours) make him feel? Forty-eight years together and in some ways, it feels like "just married." How do I separate and reconcile reality from imagined?

This I know: God has a plan, and He will reveal each part and piece to me as He decides the perfect time. He tells me to

Trust in the Lord with all my heart; do not depend on *my* own understanding. Seek his will in all *I* do, and he will show *me* which path to take. (Proverbs 3:5–6 NLT)

His light will shine on my path, He will lead me, and He promises

…I will never fail you. I will never abandon you. (Hebrews 13:5 NLT)

All will be right and good because

The Lord is my shepherd; I have all that I need. He lets me rest in green meadow; he leads me beside peaceful streams. (Psalm 23:1–2 NLT)

As I have in the past, I will, in the future, lean in, listen, follow, trust, and obey. God is good, faithful, and merciful and gives grace to those who He loves, all the time.

Reset. The season of retirement…let the walk begin!

CHAPTER 3

Progress Report

Perspective: progress report. One month and five days, what do they have to say for themselves? Interesting you should ask. Let us just say that a six-week timeline to get everything done is not being realized. The list remains with a few daily and weekly things crossed off, but those bigger items that have waited a long time to be accomplish stare me in the face, unaccomplished.

Really? What have you been doing with your time?, a small voice in my head asks. With the question out there for the world to see, I have many thoughts and mixed feelings. Impulse is to justify, and justify I do… "I am after all retired, and I do have time to get them done." Or how about, "Those are inside tasks and better suited to be done when the weather outside is, you know, frightful!" "After all, six weeks was an unreasonable expectation."

Yes, I have answers, but then there is this nagging feeling that these are just excuses, and I am feeling like a slacker. Are these feelings valid and justified? What have I been doing with my time that leaves these items on the list unaccomplished?

Weeds—remember, those things that keep growing back. Well, I have stayed on top of the task and each pulling is in less time than the first. I have maintained an appropriate weedless landscaping.

Now there is something that you all should know about me and weeds.

See, my dad was beyond perfectionist and meticulous to the nth degree about keeping his lawn and garden. He spent hours in the yard, and as a child he enlisted my help in the task. He was also the "inspector" of all my labors and frequently pointed out "you missed one there." As an adult, and no matter where I have lived, I always tried to keep our yard up to my dad's standards. To this day, working in the yard, I hear his still small voice in my head, *You missed one there*. Furthermore, my mom and her flower beds, well, let us just say, my parents were on the same team and very effective in their labors.

It has not, however, been enough to keep the landscape and gardens free of weeds; I have now started to remove weeds from the lawn. The lawn is young; it is a newer home and is, understandably, a work in progress. This is not the first time I have taken to weeding the lawn. Another thing I learned from my dad: lush green lawn, a thick carpet for bare feet, is the goal. I am impatient and naturally figure it is my job to help it along.

Now, one doesn't pull weeds 24/7, and neither do I. I may be driven, but honestly, pulling weeds, though rewarding, is simply not my favorite thing to do.

Did I mention that my mom was also a perfectionist and meticulous about keeping the home neat and clean? There is no counting the number of times as a child I was called back to redo the cleaning and dusting. Mom always said, "If you are going to do a job, do it right the first time or don't do it at all!" You guessed it; this has rattled around in my head forever. But here is the thing, as a child, my response was "Ok, I just won't do it." No, it didn't work, and I finally learned that coming back and doing the same job two or three times was just a dumb waste of time. I had much better things to do with my time, you know, like playing outside.

When I had a home of my own to care for, husband, and children, the lessons of childhood came to fruition, both in the home and in the yard. To my credit, I was awesome and excelled as a perfectionist, and some might say I have OCD about dirt, be it real or perceived. It was normal for me to clean the house five days a week, including dusting, vacuuming, mopping, and cleaning the bathrooms. Laundry was on almost as ridged of a schedule, up to three times weekly. Got to keep that laundry basket empty, don't you know?

The day came when I started working outside of the home, and there simply was no time to do things in the fashion I was used to. I tried, and oh did I try, and for a time kept up, but the demands of work, family, and church won out over cleaning, doing the laundry, and weeding. Don't get me wrong, I didn't stop cleaning, weeding, or doing laundry, I just couldn't do it every day as I was accustomed to in the past. This change was hard and did not happen overnight. Somewhere I had embraced the idea that our home had to be museum-quality clean all the time. You simply did not have company in your home if everything was not perfect. The idea that this status of perfection equaled my self-worth had deep roots in my mind and heart.

As the children got older, I enlisted their help on weekends to complete the tasks. David helped as much as he could, but often times he had to work on Saturdays, but he did a large portion of the outside yard work. But there was a problem: unlike me, my family did not embrace the "museum-quality" perspective. Déjà vu! Straight out of my childhood.

It wasn't that I was told more times than one could count, by David and others, that our home was to be lived in, my standard of perfection was unreasonable, things have changed, I need to loosen my grip, and that it's ok if there is a glass on the counter, a newspaper on the chair, and some laundry to be done. It does not all have to be done before you go to bed.

There is good news. As I have come to these days of retirement, I can boldly state that yes, the fist tight grip has been loosened. I did learn to hold life with an open palm. Company in the home has been enjoyed with dust on the coffee table. Dishes have been on the counter overnight, cleaned up in the morning, and laundry to be done in the basket, and best of all, I did not lose any sleep over it.

Back to what I have been doing this past month and five days. Yes, I have kept the house clean. We have a dog, and oh how we love our basset hound EssieMoon, but she sheds. Frequently little balls of her fur are seen drifting across the floor. If they are big enough, I will pick them up on the spot, but I manage to leave most of them for the once a week (not every day) de-furring of the floors. Laundry too is on a schedule; once a week is plenty. If Jesus returns and there is dirty laundry in the basket, He will not care. What a blessing.

Here though is the best part. In the past month, there have been days when the weather has been perfect. Those days found me in the backyard reading a book. I have completed one whole book! There have also been days when it has been beastly hot. I was in the house baking up some special treats for David. While working, I did not have much time or, for that matter, energy to do a lot of cooking. It isn't that I didn't like cooking; it was just so time- and energy-consuming. Well, the days of frozen pizza five nights in a row are behind us. I am cooking again, and I am content, even trying some new recipes, and David is ecstatic, reaping tasty rewards.

One more thing. I have always loved writing. Needless to say, time and opportunity over the years have been limited. Guess who has time now…to write! I must give this serious consideration one of these days.

This month and five days have yielded a couple of other important things: First and foremost, the reassurance that my self-worth comes solely from God, my Heavenly Father. I am who I am, not because of what I have done, but because of what God has done in and through me.

Retirement does not render me useless, unneeded. In His kindness, mercy, and love for me, God has given me opportunities to help others, in this short, one month and five days.

I am still seeking purpose for my life in retirement. I know it is more than pulling weeds, cleaning, doing laundry, and cooking, though I am glad for the time to indulge in these activities. God also confirmed to me that He has a purpose for my life in retirement by pointing out one thing that it is not. A friend kindly suggested getting involved in a senior center; I could play Bridge or Bingo and have a social time.

The conversation with David went something like, "I am not going waste my time playing Bingo! I have more left in me to give and to do. If Bingo is all I have left, I might as well be dead!" No offense to my friend who is nigh unto ten years older. It is right for them and they enjoy it. I'm just not there yet.

God has made it clear that I need to take care of myself and engage in things that will nurture my mind, body, spirit, and soul. Retirement is time for self-maintenance, taking time to care for things that have been neglected. Assignment: loose the guilt over relaxation and establish, discipline, and maintain scheduled self-improvement of body, mind, spirit, and soul. Breathe deep, exhale slow, smile, and enjoy. Never doubt how much your Father loves you.

> Long ago the Lord said to Israel; "I have loved you, my people, with an everlasting love. With unfailing love, I have drawn you to myself." (Jeremiah 31:3 NLT)

God still speaks these words to us today.

CHAPTER 4

Time Flies

Perspective: time flies! Welcome back! Six months and twenty days into retirement, and it is the dead of winter. As I reviewed the first month and five days, it occurred to me that I have not recorded a single word for five months and fifteen days! How is retirement working for me now?

A blow by blow is not necessary, but a few highlights seem worthy.

The month of August brought friends from France and a week of travel including visits with family on the return home. September brought to fruition an item from "the list" to socialize, meet new people, and study the Bible, thus creating a small but significant routine, which lasted through mid-November. Two months of holidays, prep, participation, and clean-up. Once the holiday clean-up was accomplished, I knocked off five more tasks from "the list." Interspersed into these months, I completed two more books, cooked up a storm, and ventured a small creative outlet, not yet completed…oh, and yes, permission to enjoy, briefly, a few opportunities to…do nothing and rest.

In all honesty, though accomplishments have been made, I am still in the learning curve.

A new month, year, and decade give birth to new beginnings, fresh starts, and possibilities.

> "For I know the plans I have for you," says the Lord, "They are plans for good and not for disaster, to give you a future and a hope." (Jeremiah 29:11 NLT)

Many times, along the path of my life, God has reassured me with these very words, and once again, He speaks hope and possibility to my heart, and I receive and embrace the promise.

Sounds simple, but when you live in my head, it is not. I am a tad OCD proactive in most everything I set out to accomplish. Here, the word "plan" plants a visual aide in my mind. A long list (imagine that) of steps move me from the beginning to the end seamlessly. I read through the list and get a mental overview picture of what lies ahead and then dive in headfirst. Let's get this started. My eagerness to accomplish the most in the least amount of time explodes and threatens to consume me.

> "My thoughts (*plans KJV*) are nothing like your thoughts," (*plans KJV*) says the Lord. "And my ways are far beyond anything you could imagine. For just as the heavens are higher than the earth, so are my ways higher than your ways and my thoughts (*plans KJV*) higher than your thoughts." (*plans KJV*) (Isaiah 55:8–9 NLT)

This is simply God pushing the "hold" button on my mind and heart as He gently encourages me to stop, breathe, exhale, and listen.

Just after my head hits the pillow at night, and I am not quite ready to fall asleep, the quiet provides the perfect time to talk, or just listen, to my Heavenly Father. Of recent it has gone something like this.

"Father, I am not old, and I still have a lot of life to live and give. I don't know what that looks like, but I am ready. I want to do what You want for me, so what is it?"

You probably notice some impatience, and you are right. God noticed too and told me, "Just close your eyes and go to sleep."

"But…"

"I love you, and now it's time to sleep."

Sadly, I must admit, we did not have this conversation just once since the start of the New Year.

Twenty days into the month, most of my winter, in-house "to do's" on "the list" have been moved to the "done" side, and yes, I am feeling accomplished but also staring down the barrel of "what's next." I am thinking, *Where can I volunteer, what would I like to do, maybe I should look for something part time*. My thoughts then drift to, *Oh, but it's winter, and it's cold, and I really don't want to "have to" go out and do something*. Scratch that idea! Maybe just get some good books to read. Nice but a bit lame. Activity, you need some activity, the dog needs walking, and you were doing so good getting out for a walk every day. But it is really cold, and I do not want to, much less have to, do cold.

So, I keep asking, "Father, what is your plan for me now?"

On the way to church Sunday morning, sitting in the warm vehicle on my toasty heated seat, I stared out the window at the barren, snow-covered and cold fields. God says to me, "Write."

"Write?"

"Yes, you like to write."

"Sure, but what do I write about? What do I know anything about anything?"

"Write about what you know best, you."

"Where would I begin, and what would I say? I'm not interesting. And besides, if I write, should it not be something that is useful, helpful, including and glorifying to You Father, and that benefits the reader?"

"I will guide you."

My Heavenly Father does not accept my self-criticism, which is more to the tune of an insulting slap in His face, and I was promptly corrected with this reminder.

Oh Lord, you have examined my heart and know everything about me. You know when I sit down or stand up. You know my thoughts even when I'm far away. You see me when I travel and when I rest at home. You know everything I do. You know what I am going to say even before I say it, Lord. You go before me and follow me. You place your hand of blessing on my head. Such knowledge is too wonderful for me, too great for me to understand! I can never escape from your Spirit! I can never get away from your presence! If I go up to heaven, you are there; if I go down to the grave, you are there. If I ride the wings of the morning, if I dwell by the farthest oceans, even there your hand will guide me, and your strength will support me. I could ask the darkness to hide me and the light around me to become night—but even in darkness I cannot hide from you. To you the night shines as bright as day. Darkness and light are the same to you. You made all the delicate, inner parts of my body and knit me together in my mother's womb. Thank you for making me so wonderfully complex! Your workmanship is marvelous—how well I know it. You watched me as I was being formed in utter seclusion, as I was woven together in the dark of the womb. You saw me before I was born. Every day of my life was recorded in your book. Every moment was laid out before a single day had passed.

How precious are your thoughts about me, O God. They cannot be numbered! I can't even count them; they outnumber the grains of sand! And when I wake up, you are still with me! (Psalm 139:1–18 NLT)

…search me, O God, and know my heart; test me and know my anxious thoughts. Point out anything in me that offends you, and lead me along the path of everlasting life. (Psalm 139:23–24 NLT)

Tears welled up in my eyes, a lump of guilt in my throat, a confession of wrong attitude on my lips, I sought forgiveness for my heart and received it with His enduring words of "I love you, Carol."

Here is to "new beginnings," "fresh starts," and a venture into the unknown. I have no idea what will fill the coming pages, but I know God does.

Your word is a lamp to guide my feet and light for my path. (Psalm 119:105 NLT)

What I do know about myself is that my life has been a walk of faith, stepping out into unknowns because God told me to. God has never been wrong, and I know He will not be now.

Retirement! Let the adventure begin!

CHAPTER 5

Unexpected Changes

Perspective: unexpected changes. Over my lifetime, I have worked fifty plus years, starting when I was thirteen with babysitting. Variety would best describe the kinds of work and jobs I have invested my time and energy into.

A quick review: baby sitter, clerk/sales at a dry cleaners, floral shop, lady's clothing store/fabric/home accessories; customer service, switchboard operator/receptionist, magazine/newspaper proofreader; fast food prep/sales; professional home packer/mover; accounts receivable/payables, telephone sales; medical office scheduler; assistant manager retail store; radio advertising, sales, and broadcast; international sales, personnel director assistant; nursing home department manager; legal assistant; retail business owner; elementary school administrative assistant; and interspersed through all of it, wife, mother, and homemaker.

Additionally, I was involved in church and ministry. Choir, Awana, Sunday school teacher and superintendent, church and Christian School Boards of Education, church facility expansion, church board, missions, hospitality committees, Women's Ministries, local Christian Women's Club, and Bible study leader.

I woke up one morning, retired. Overnight my life drastically changed. Not unexpected, we had been planning this day for over three years. What came next though was never even a spec on my radar.

First was the insurance reality. For years I carried the health insurance. My husband's needs are significant, and the insurance was awesome. Gone. Both being of Medicare age, it became our next glaring reality. Yes, we knew it was coming and had planned for it, but somehow it did not sink in, until it sank in.

Next was my paycheck. Gone. Now yes, I have a retirement pension and of course social security, but somehow, "security" weakens at this point. To explain seems elusive, but there is some-thing very real about the feeling.

Daily social interaction. Gone. I had people, families, children, and coworkers that I served every day. Service to others, many others, gives meaning, purpose, definition, opportunities, satisfac-tion, accomplishment, and more. Gone. Yes, they are still there, and they still have needs, but someone else is taking care of, dare I say, my family, my peeps. It is like being on the other side of the window, looking in. There is sadness and sense of loss.

Work, actually, daily responsibilities. Familiar, routine, functions performed automatically, with little thought, offering direction, scheduling my time, organizing my daily routine. Gone. As much as I love "not my problem anymore," I miss the challenge and the energy that is generated and the satisfaction it produces.

Routine, tedious as it may be, partnered with a schedule you would give anything to deviate from. Gone. One would think this would be cause for great rejoicing! I find myself floundering.

Early morning drive to work as the world is just waking up and the sun is rising. Often, I just wanted to stop by the side of the road and watch the miracle and beauty of a new day unfold before my eyes, but I could not take the time. Gone. I ask myself why, because this one does not have to be, but it is. I lay this fault square at my own feet. This change is actually one that would not have to be, at least not every day.

No one asks for help. Not that they don't need it, or even that they can actually figure it out themselves. No one wants to burden me, or interfere with my days of newfound freedom. *This is your time now*, they say, *enjoy it, we can handle things*. Being needed. Gone.

Pressure, stress, weariness at the end of the day, feeling overwhelmed, buried, cannot breathe, fear of forgetting something, letting someone down, always being on call. Gone. Ah, that is a good thing Carol, is it not? I don't understand it either.

Now some might say, "Carol you should have known these things," and in a way, I did, but like so much of life, you do not really "know" until you have literally walked down that path. Knowing something intellectually is different, in a big way, from living it daily, moment to moment, having firsthand experience.

But then came a "big" one that really threw me for a loop. For Medicare you have to have this annual wellness check. Ok, I get it, they want to know up front what your issues are, and a yearly checkup was not foreign to me, so hey, no big deal, right? Wrong. Well, maybe not for everyone, but for me, it was wrong,

Now at times, I admit, I can be naïve. I am going through this normal checkup, all is good, and then these questions start coming. At first, I thought, *Ok something new, just go with it*. Then they asked me, "Do you have a bar in your shower?" Without skipping a beat, I answered, "No, why would I, I don't drink in the shower!" They proceeded to ask, "Do you have a stool in your shower?" Again, I answered, "No, it's a shower. I don't sit, I stand!" Finally, they asked me, "Do you feel safe in your home?" *Seriously!* I thought but said, "This is demeaning and insulting."

Well, I am sure by now you get it. They explained to me that because I was now retired and because of my age, these questions were required for processing me with Medicare. At this point they seemed to back off a bit and skipped some of the questions, but I did have to draw a clock and show them 8:20 on the clock. I was revved up by now and said, "Sure, I will show you how elementary school children tell time today." I promptly drew a box and put 8:20 in it. Everything in their world is digital. They gave me this look, and I said, "Fine," drew the circle, put in the numbers, and then drew the hands to reflect 8:20.

I sputtered to God all the way home. "I am not old, feeble, senile, helpless, or abused. I am not even a month retired, and they are treating me like I should be headed for the nursing home next week. Oh, Father God, I am angry and upset." My knee jerk reaction was kicking in, and I knew it. I should have been more docile and nice, after all they are just doing their job, but my switch was flipped, and I was in react mode.

"Why did you make me this way, God? Independent, strong-willed, stubborn, knee jerk reactive!" I could hardly believe what my Heavenly Father replied to my question, but I cherish it: "Because I love you, for your protection, to help you stretch and grow." A personality trait I have dealt with all my life was intentionally gifted to me my loving Heavenly Father, for my benefit. This was and is a lot to digest, but as I take glances back on my life, the light of understanding keeps turning on.

Retirement's unexpected changes. There is a lot more unexplored territory than I ever imagined. My journey is not over; it is just beginning, again, a new start, new opportunities, and new chapter. With the new comes reflections of what has been and questions of what is to come. *What was* helps us understand *what is* and prepares us for that which is yet to come. A three-fold journey I invite you to share with me.

> For everything there is a season, a time for every activity under heaven. (Ecclesiastes 3:1 NLT)

CHAPTER 6

Beginnings

Perspective: beginnings. We all start somewhere, and for me, what I believe was my beginning is found in scripture.

I knew you before I formed you in your mother's womb… (Jeremiah 1:5 NLT)

You watched me as I was being formed in utter seclusion, as I was woven together in the dark of the womb. (Psalms 139:16 NLT)

I also believe that I am an intentional masterpiece with a purpose.

For I *am* God's masterpiece. He has created *me* anew in Christ Jesus, so *I* can do good things he planned for *me* long ago. (Ephesians 2:10 NLT)

Many times, throughout my life when I was anxious and even fearful of "what is next," I found these to be anchors of reassurance, direction, and purpose. God knows and He has a plan.

My earthly trek began in the newly constructed hospital in Fort Atkinson, Wisconsin, where my parents lived, at 1:00 am on the first day of spring, March 21. The year I was born, it was the first day of spring, and for me, so shall it always be. My mother told me that a tornado tore through the mid part of our state that night; we however were not in its path. I have long affectionately embraced my stormy debut, and as my life unfolded, it seemed appropriate.

Being born on the first day of spring has always been monumentally special to me, and I will argue with anyone who now dares to say my birthday is no longer the first day of spring. Spring is my favorite season of the year. Winter is finally gone, and the earth gives birth to all things new, fresh, and alive.

I am awed at the lace-like leaves as they are just spreading their wings on the tree branches. Their color is especially vibrant and their structure soft and delicate yet determined. Grass is the greenest in spring, and nothing compares to the smell of freshly mowed grass. Spring flowers, strong, sturdy, unyielding as they push their way up through the ground giving way to fragrant, colorful blooms. All this budding forth fills the air with God's sweet fragrances. Oh, if only that "pause" button would work, I would extend these precious warm sunny moments.

Spring surrounds you with the hope of life, new beginnings, and fresh starts. Hope is witnessed by anyone who drives through the countryside and sees farmers plowing the fields and planting the seeds. Anticipation of new life ignites the air. Soil has a special scent that waifs across the landscape urging you to get your hands dirty. So grand is this overture of life that even I have delusions of growing anything and everything. Garden centers become my preferred destination where lofty dreams are quickly grounded by the reality that my thumbs are not inherently green. The few plants I do have are meticulously cared for, just like my dad taught me.

Every birthday I am reminded that life has new beginnings, second chances, fresh starts, new horizons, and opportunities to stretch and grow. The struggles are real and the storms can be fierce, but my Heavenly Father whispers to me,

(I Am) God is *my* refuge and strength, always ready to help in times of trouble. (Psalm 46:1 NLT)

The first of my beginnings laid the foundation for the person I have become. God graciously gave me a solid foundation on which to build a life. He placed me in a home where reading the Bible and praying together as a family were a daily essential. Though not perfect (thank heaven), my parents loved me and did their best with what they had to meet my spiritual, physical, social, emotional, material, and educational needs. By no means were we rich in earthly treasures, but we were rich in family; church community; traditions; simple pleasures; rewards of hard work; opportunities to learn, stretch, and grow (though at times I was certain this was not true); and a sense of security, love, and belonging. Perhaps at the time I did not fully appreciate just how rich my life was, but today, looking back, I am assured that the foundation of my life was secure.

Birth: the beginning of one's life, the start of a journey, a world of possibilities. The importance of each new beginning experienced in life is measured by the perspective of the individual. As we mature, perspective changes, and life experiences are the initiator of the change.

There are things I just do not remember about my life. Between the age of birth to three or so, I doubt I was conscious of the many changes that took place. Parents on the other hand live for those moments of change. As a parent I remember well those changes in my own children. They are nothing short of gifts and miracles from God, and they are fresh and new with each child.

I have memory of the days prior to kindergarten, the dreaded afternoon nap that seemed like such a total waste of playtime. Looking back, they were important. Was it motherly wisdom, just a given, a mom's need for a break? Time proved that, for me, they were a healthy necessity as I frequently got sick when overtired.

The best thing about pre-kindergarten was freedom, and I understood this well, freedom to play in the sandbox and ride my tricycle (or my sister's when she was in school; it was bigger, faster, and red!). We had a playroom in our basement for those cold days. No matter where I played, I was the ultimate "pretender." My adventures were awesome, equaling my very creative imagination! The worst part of any day was having to stop to eat and sleep.

One of my most vivid and certainly most important beginning in life (though I did not grasp its importance, or that it was a beginning, at the time) came when I was just four years old. It was my routine to watch Captain Kangaroo in the morning while mom was upstairs making beds and tidying up. This one morning in particular as the program was coming to a close, Captain Kangaroo said, "...so children, be sure to say your prayers so one day you will go to the right place."

I was nine days old when my parents took me to church for the first time. I started Sunday school at the age of two. Cannot say I remember much about it, but one thing that was firm in my understanding was that Jesus loved me and that He wanted to live in my heart. All I had to do was confess my sins and ask Him to come into my heart, and He would forgive me and I would be saved for eternity. Was not really clear on my sins or that eternity concept, but ok, I was good with it.

That morning I went upstairs and found my mom in my sister's bedroom. I told her that I wanted to go to heaven when I died, and Captain Kangaroo said I had to say my prayers to make that happen. I told my mom that I wanted to make that happen. We sat on the side of my sister's bed and in terms a four-year old could understand, my mom explained the plan of salvation to me. Then she asked me if I was ready to invite Jesus into my heart, and I said yes. We kneeled down next to my sister's bed, and mom told me to repeat a prayer after her. She prayed, and I repeated, and that morning Jesus came into my heart and life to live. My parting thought was, *Ok, that is taken care of. A seed was planted.*

The reality of the impact this decision would make on my life was acquired as I grew in knowledge and understanding and continues to impact my life every day that I live.

Then came my first dramatic, conscious, new beginning: kindergarten. I suppose most children get excited over the prospect of starting school, but not me. So many new rules: early bedtime, early rise and shine; care to be taken about the clothing I was to put on; hygiene, making sure I was clean, my hair combed, and my teeth brushed; and even breakfast became a burden. I had to eat it all and eat it fast. Perhaps my given nickname explains a lot, "poke pants."

All that before I even left the house. Enter "the clock"! My life was now ordered by the school bell. Now understand, my school was right across the street, a two-minute walk, at most. I was never late, but trust me, I was never early. Slipping in the door as the bell was ringing suited me just fine, much to my mother's dismay.

School also brought all those kids. Yes, most kids would eat this up, but not me. I was a habitual daydreamer, and trust me, a room full of kids was a major distraction. Not to mention "the teacher." She had her own agenda and set of rules, which I confess, I learned quickly because the alternative was not user-friendly.

Please understand, it wasn't all bad. I had four favorite things that I loved about kindergarten: story time, coloring pictures (the smell of crayons), singing songs, and rest time. I lived for these moments in my day. You get a lot of daydreaming done during rest time, and the other three fed my imagination.

I did not enjoy recess, and yes that sounds strange, but here is the thing. I loved going off on my own and playing by myself; my imagination was well equipped with adventures. But the adults on the playground did not find this appropriate. Recess was a time to play with other kids and learn the social skills of sharing, respect, team work, and cooperation. Perhaps I gave off a certain vibe, but all those kids didn't seem to like me much, and I noticed. Playing alone spared hurt feelings, mine.

Back in the day when I was in kindergarten, we only went half days, and my half was in the morning. Now, afternoons would have suited me much better for two reasons: I was not a morning person, and, even though I was in kindergarten, I still had to take that stupid nap after lunch. That really cut into my freedom to play, and I did not adjust well to this new lifestyle.

I do have two particular memories of my year in kindergarten. I don't know why, but for some reason we had to take these "goiter" pills. What purpose they served, I still, to this day, have no idea. But their flavor was chocolate! We would line up by this closet door, the teacher would stand there holding the bag of goiter pills, and we were to reach in and take one, put it in our mouth, and eat it right away. Confession, they taste good, and I never took just one.

My second memory was the day during rest time, the girl next to me said, "You have spots on your arms." I firmly denied it, but she insisted, and she told the teacher! Now for some reason, I did not want to go home. I don't remember why, but if I were to guess, one of my favorite things was next after rest time. Upon examining my arms, I was packed up and sent to the office where my mother came and picked me up. It was valid; I had scarlatina. Not exactly sure what that was; I just remember having a fever, red spots that appeared and disappeared, and having to rest all day long, and I threw up once on the living room floor. I still remember my dad cleaning it up while finishing his hamburger. That was just gross in my five-year-old mind. My great aunt Luella brought me daffodils to brighten my day and a book, *Peppy: The Lonely Little Puppy*. To this day, I love daffodils, and that book was one of my all-time favorites.

I was ecstatic when school got out for the summer and I was looking forward the three whole months of freedom. Summer must be as close to heaven as one came, and at the ripe old age of six, I thought I was in heaven. But even heaven had a cloud. Often the thought crossed my mind that school was my lot in life for the next twelve years. At the age of six, this most certainly was an eternity, and so my perspective was formed.

I was in elementary school for the next six years, and those years were loaded with ups and downs for me. My elementary school-related highlights remain with me today. I absolutely love reading books and listening to someone read to me. My older sister was a reader, and many Saturday mornings I would crawl into bed with her before breakfast, and she would read to me.

Teachers would have a time of reading while we sat quietly eating our snack and drinking the most marvelous chocolate milk from a glass bottle. There were times when students were asked to read to the class. Some kids would agonize over this honor, but I loved it, because I could read well. Between my love of reading and chocolate, this time became my all-time favorite.

I also enjoyed spelling and was very good at it. We would have classroom spelling bees using that week's list of spelling words. Sides were chosen, and we had a competition between the two teams. I mention this because this was the only time in my life that I was one of the first to be chosen for the team. I was an excellent speller, and I was actually wanted on a team. When teams were picked for kick ball, soft ball, or any other kind of sport, I was always the last one picked for the team. I was not good at sports, and everyone knew it.

I loved art and music, and these classes remained at the top of my list of things I enjoyed in school. Physical education on the other hand ranked at the bottom every time. I was not good at it; kids knew it and made fun of me, and the teacher was a bit of a hard-nosed critical person which certainly did nothing for raising my enthusiasm for the class. I remember thinking she must be a very unhappy person as she rarely smiled and was always stern.

Math and science were ok. I was better in math so naturally enjoyed it more. But my favorite was social studies, or basically history with some geography thrown in. For me the seeds were planted early and have continued to grow throughout my lifetime. My love for history is right up there with chocolate. There is just something priceless about knowing where we came from, what we went through to achieve were we are today.

For some reason I found afternoons in elementary school long and boring. We would go home for an hour at lunch time, and my mom always had our big meal then. Perhaps it was all that good food settling into my stomach that made afternoons a challenge to remain alert and attentive. I well remember frequently having my mom's homemade dill pickles for lunch. I would save it to last, and then the last bite I tucked securely in my cheek and kept it there until returning home at the end of school. Throughout the afternoon, I would give it just a small little bite to refresh its wonderful flavor of dill pickle in my mouth.

The last minutes of every day in elementary school, we would pack up and prepare to go home. Bus students always left five minutes before the bell so they could catch their bus. I would watch the second hand on the clock ever so slowly make its rounds five times until the click to three o'clock, at which time the most glorious sound ever would occur—the end of day bell.

Other things were interspersed into the elementary times of first conscious beginnings in my life that were not connected to school, but with family. My grandma and grandpa lived on a farm and raised Guernsey cows. They also raised sheep, had two horses, turkeys, geese, ducks and chickens. I absolutely loved the farm! Going to grandma's made Friday the perfect end to the school week. I spent every weekend and as many weeks in the summer that I possibly could out on the farm.

The farm had so much to offer that living in town could not: farm animals. I had my own special cow; her name was Miriam. She was not the greatest producer, but she was sweet and gentle. Her stanchion was along the aisle where I could brush, feed, and milk her. Grandma had this tin cup that I could strip milk into. Warm milk straight from the cow was a special treat. During the summer when she was out in the pasture, I could walk right up to her or sit next to her without concern. Grandma kept her around just for me until she was just too old.

Grandpa had two Belgian draft horses, Bell and Betsy. They towered over me, but when grandpa was around, I could help lead them, give them treats, and ride the wagon they pulled. Many times, calves, lambs, and kids (baby goats) were bottle-fed, and I was always available to help out. You have not seen joy until you have seen the tail of these little ones wiggling while feasting on milk.

Living in town, the only thing I could enter through 4H was baked goods and sewing projects. That was my sister's area of expertise, not mine. I was not able to show animals at the County Fair through 4H, but that never stopped me from training them in the farmyard. Once though I did assist my uncle at the State Fair when he entered his twin goats, Flash and Flipper. I was in the ring showing Flash and took Grand Champion.

Grandma's chickens, ducks, geese, and turkeys I viewed from a distance. The chickens and turkeys were in their coops and were just too clucky and flighty to go near for my taste. The ducks and geese had the run of the farmyard, and I learned quickly to not cross their path; they were very territorial. The only time I enjoyed the bird population was when grandma had them as babies in her kitchen under the warming lights.

It was not just the animals that I enjoyed on the farm. The farm has chores, and I actually liked doing farm chores, such as feeding the cows, sheep, goats, and horses, cleaning the barn (yes, shoveling manure), washing up the milking machines, cleaning the milk house, helping with milk test samples, mowing the lawn with an old push mower, weeding the garden, pumping water from the cistern, and, yes, helping grandma in the kitchen and cleaning her house.

When I was old enough, I was allowed to go up the lane to the pastures and woods or sit on the hill that overlooked the farm and do my favorite thing—daydream. Often, we would gather hickory nuts and wild black berries and help grandma cook up special treats. Grandma gave me my own plot of ground for a garden, and she let me grow anything I wanted, and she helped me be a success in my endeavors. Just beyond the garden was the field of sugarcane. Every fall I would help grandma harvest by hand the sugarcane which was loaded up and taken to a processing place where the best sorghum (a lot like molasses) was the end product. Sorghum on homemade bread could almost replace chocolate.

My grandma, like most, was an awesome cook, and there was no end to her making all my favorites, from chocolate milk to hot dishes, and breakfast topped my list of favorites with homemade bread for toast, coco wheats, fresh eggs, or bologna from the market in town.

I was drawn to the farm machinery, and sometimes too much so that grandma would chase me away because I was too young. Grandpa would let me ride on the tractor with him, and if grandma caught us, she would scold. Then came the day that I was old and big enough to actually drive the tractor, always under grandpa's watchful eye, but I felt so accomplished.

Grandpa also had his workshop that had everything you could imagine or not imagine. I loved to build things, and grandpa would give me scraps of this and that, and under his watchful eye, he helped to create things out of almost nothing. I remember fondly the boat he helped me build, and then we fashioned a paddle, and I sailed it around the big round, cement watering tank in the cow yard next to the barn. Grandma was always concerned that I would fall in, and her warnings instilled a sense of safety in me.

The smells on the farm, perhaps for most, are not pleasing, but I loved the smell of the barn, the horses, the silage in the silo, the fresh-cut hay, the sweetness of the apple orchard, and nothing compared to the smell of the wood furnace or grandmas wood stove. Many evenings grandpa would make fresh hot buttered popcorn on that old wooden stove.

We had many family gatherings to celebrate holidays and birthdays. In addition, we would get together at grandma's farm to pick hickory nuts and black berries, go on hay wagon rides, picnics in the woods, tobogganing down the hill, and, often, just because. Family ties were strong, and most of my family on both sides growing up lived in the same town and went to the same church. Nowadays, family connections such as I had growing up are not so common, even in my own family. As we grew up, life has taken us in many different directions, but I will always cherish the memories I have of my days on the farm.

My perspective, by the age of twelve, was largely shaped by my home, family, and church. Life was simpler, easier to understand. Bumps in the path played their part in my life, but because the foundation was solid, much that today is dramatic drama just did not happen. Did I feel less hurt? Not really. Was I an angel? Certainly not! Analyzing everything did not seem necessary to achieve understanding. Looking back, I am certain, God used every experience to form and shape me. Nothing wasted, everything purposeful.

CHAPTER 7

Growing Up

Perspective: growing up. A little older, a bit wiser, I entered junior high. This in part was another beginning. All the students from each elementary school were now all together under one roof, so there were new students to meet. Gone were the classrooms where we had one teacher all day. Now, for each subject we moved to a different room with a different teacher, and each day started in "homeroom." The concept was a bit scary, but the challenge was refreshing and the days passed quickly.

The basic subjects were still in place but stepped up. Science became "biology," math became "algebra," reading and spelling evolved into "English," and music became "choir" or "band." I chose choir. Physical education had another dimension, "health." Art was still art, but the projects were more advanced and challenging. Boys could do shop, girls had home economics, and library was actually part of the schedule together with study hall. Lunch was shorter and everyone stayed at school, and recess was nonexistent.

Over all the subjects were more challenging, homework became a daily thing, and social life revolved around your locker. As we got used to each other, new friendships took root, some old ones faded, and the opposite sex took on new meaning.

Junior high is a transition period of life in so many ways. Mix all those changes with the hormonal changes that manifested in each of us, and we became a colorful mix of drama, fun, and emotions, testing the waters of adventure and independence.

Those days, parents did not drive their kids to school every day or pick them up after school. My two-minute stroll across the street turned into a jaunt of over a mile, one way, every day. This was a major crimp in my morning routine. Only if it was pouring rain did mom take dad to work so she could drive us to school. If the rain ended by the time school was out, we walked. If it was cold out, we wore pants over heavy tights, extra socks inside our boots, and hats and scarfs that covered our heads (well, at least as long as I was in eye shot of home). Changing in and out of all that bundling was nothing short of just being a major annoyance. It seems that backpacks had not yet been invented as I carried all of my books in my arms, or at best in a large bag; at least that was my experience. Neither was very comfortable or convenient. Many days my arms and back ached from the load.

Parent–teacher conferences were held with the homeroom teacher. In seventh grade I had an awesome homeroom teacher, Mr. Wildermuth. He was young, tall, thin, full of energy, always smiling, and, apparently, very perceptive also. After their first conference with him, my parents came home and told me that Mr. Wildermuth said they had a strong-willed independent daughter. Imagine that! To this day, I love it!

I think my parents knew this full well, and it just kept getting reinforced as I continue through high school. My older sister, whom I dearly love, and I were different. For example, if my parents were to ask her to jump, she would ask, "How high would you like me to jump?" But ask me the same question, my reply would be, "Give me a good reason to do so." That was true of my sister back then. Today, she would be asking for a good reason also.

Looking at the strong women we come from, I'd say independent strength is in our DNA.

My sister was an honor student, got good grades, and earned a silver cord at graduation. She went on to technical school for one year right after high school to become a medical assistant. Upon graduation she started working in our family doctor's office. Our parents were proud of her accomplishments.

Repeatedly, coming home after parent–teacher conferences, my parents shared with me that they had been told, "She is not her sister." This impacted my life for years to come. I expect my parents were fully aware that I was not like my sister but secretly hoped I might follow her example. Here was my take on this evaluation of me. "That is right, I am not my sister; I am me, and do not expect me to be like her." Whereas my sister excelled in school, I made it through with mostly Cs, a few Ds and Bs, and occasionally an A. My goal was to just get to graduation and be done with this thirteen-year sentence. I was always looking forward to the day of freedom when I could just be me. This line of self-definition drawn in the sand would not stop at high school graduation. I would come to invest a lot of energy into expounding my own individuality, ultimately desiring to just be accepted and appreciated for who and what I was, which was not bad, simply different.

Stepping away for a moment for some forward looking into my post-high school adult life. My sister (as is natural, she was older) proceeded me. She had been there, done that, before I arrived. The impact was specific. Coming into new situations, meeting new people, I became known as, "Oh, you are Sandy's sister." Whether it was true or not, it felt to me that being recognize as "Sandy's sister" was the only point of reference others had of me. This upset me, a lot. I was not upset with my sister; it wasn't her fault. I was upset because I had no identity. This did not bode well with the independent sort that I was.

I had a real need to feel recognized and accepted, but for me. The need impacted the way I dressed, the things I did, choices I made, and people I engaged, but strangely, not always to stand out, but to fit in. I still brought my perspective and pieces of myself to each situation, but I really believed the lie that I was only accepted because of the efforts I made to "fit in." Even later, when my sister moved away, and the comparison seemed less, I felt there were certain things that must be done to fit in.

Then one day, an older, much wiser woman took me under her wing. Mind you, she was a woman wise in the ways of the world; savvy in business, investments, and social graces; and skilled in reading and knowing people. Why she took a liking to me, I don't know, except that this was a Divine appointment. We did things together, and she took time to get to know "me"! One day she said to me, "Honey, who is pulling your strings?" I asked her what she meant, and she informed me that it was obvious I was trying to be someone I clearly was not. All she advised was, "Honey, it's time to cut the strings and be yourself."

She saw something worthy in me, just me. It still brings tears to my eyes, but I have carried her advice with me and have allowed God to use it, allowing me to bloom, spread my wings, and become.

My mom and I disagreed on many aspects of life, from music, how things were done, to how we each saw the world and the people in it. Mom was a strong woman, very opinionated, and did not pull any punches when sharing her views on my perceptions, life choices, and views. Somewhere in my mid-30s, apparently, we both softened a bit. The nature of our conversations became more understanding and accepting. As we picked our way through various topics, we both admitted that we could see why and value in the way the other felt. Many points of disagreement were nothing more than the times and circumstances in which we each were raised. On some issues mom even conceded that she just had not experienced things from my perspective because when she was my age, either information was not available or people just did not discuss or question. There were consequences for her if she did not do what she was told that I had zero exposure to. Back then, she was taught to accept things and do what she was told, and she did. As God stretched and grew her, she learned to stand her ground.

Though we never did fully agree with each other on everything, we both learned new things about each other. We developed a healthy ability to respect our differences, accept that on some things, neither of us would change and agreeing to disagree was ok. Issues of conflict between us had more to do with personality, personal likes and dislikes, and the place each of us were in life. Our issues were never threatening, life-and-death, or law breaking. What a blessing to become more than mother and daughter—we became friends. We shared a lot of our lives, feelings, and experiences. I know there were things that I kept private, and after my mother's death, I became aware that she, too, kept some things private. To this day I don't know the full extent of what my mother experienced in her lifetime, but I do know, it did not break her—it made her stronger, a legacy that she passed on to me.

Back now… High school brought to me a few more "firsts." I held a couple of part-time jobs after school and earned my own money, to do with as I chose. Sniff that freedom! Passing the test, the first time, and getting my driver's license! Loved it, more freedom, and oh, so sweet, independence and speed (even if I had to use my dad's car), but I had money and could put gas in the tank. Dating. My mother said I was "boy crazy," but here's the thing, the boys drove cool cars, and the only one I dated in high school drove cool cars. He graduated two years before me, and it did not last long, but it sure was fun. I will admit, my parents had a right to be concerned. Though the only boy I dated was very nice, and from a nice family, I really liked the "bad boys." Now none of them gave me the time of day, which was probably good, but it didn't stop me from looking.

Now mind you, just because the wilder side of life is what fascinated me, I still lived a sheltered life, was still naïve, and had few opportunities to indulge. Even if I had the opportunities, there existed inside of me a still but very strong voice, discerning right from wrong. It was Jesus, living in me and keeping me.

Well, this beginning came to a close on graduation day. Went to bed one night a senior in high school and woke up the next day breathing the first breath of eighteen-year-old freedom! Push the "pause" button, and cherish the moment—it too was fleeting.

CHAPTER 8

Life Post-High School

Perspective: life, adventure, and post-high school. Unlike many of my classmates, I did not go on to college or even technical school. Honestly, thirteen years of school, I simply had enough and I wanted to move onto something new. For me, that something new was a job.

A friend of my mom managed a women's clothing store, Neiperts, that also handled fabric and sewing supplies as well as household accessories. The store had been on the same corner of Main Street for as long as I could remember, and the owner, Mr. Neipert, lived upstairs above the store. Working as a clerk in this store was my first job out of high school. Another girl from my graduating class also worked there, and though we had not been friends in school, we became friendly.

I enjoyed the older women who worked in the store. They were fun, experienced, and had a perspective of life I had yet to learn and was eager to do so. I was taught how to be a window dresser, and I loved the creativity this allowed me. Soon I was put in charge of the whole lower level and I enjoyed the independence.

Things changed though after this one day when my boss, the store manager, was trying on clothes and asked my opinion. Now mind you, she was my mother's age, but she put on leather and fringes, something you might expect a "hippie" of the 1970s to wear. She did not seem to appreciate my honesty when I told her I thought she looked better when she dressed in clothes her own age. Soon afterward she became more critical of my work and even had conversations with my mother about my attitude. It was not rocket science to see the writing on the wall, and we soon parted ways.

Perspective is influenced by characteristics of a person. This was of memory, my first realization of one of my characteristics. What you see is what you get. It is written on my face, carried on my shoulders, and expressed through my mouth and body language. Just because I was nineteen when this happened, do not think for one moment, it is gone. I have invested a lifetime of learning to manage appropriately this characteristic. It is double-sided, awesome in some cases, and a disaster in others.

It has been no small matter in my life of constantly surrendering this to God. It would have been much easier if God would have just removed it from me, but as I look back on my life, it has been one of His greatest tools for molding and shaping me into the person I am today. What sometimes felt like a curse has truly been a blessing, and I am thankful for the way it has kept me close to my Heavenly Father. I am reminded of a song, often sung at the end of the church service when I was growing up, "All to Jesus, I Surrender. All to Him I freely give. I will ever love and trust Him, in His presence daily live."

I was not unemployed long and soon landed a job in the customer service department of a local farm supply business, Nasco, which also had an art, home economics, biology, live material, plastics, and medical divisions, along with branches in California that handled guns and ammunition. I had my own desk, typewriter, and phone and handle customer issues from all over the United States. I was responsible for all aspects of the customer service, from tracking shipments to replacing lost or damaged items, filing claims, placing orders, tracking and filing all my own paperwork, and utilizing all forms of communications from written to direct phone customer contact. The variety of the work was challenging and inspiring. I love the contact with people, coworkers, and customers.

It was here that I learned what really floated my boat—helping others. I poured my heart into my work, loving the relationship opportunities afforded me with people and grew to a place where I understood how to successfully relate to people. There was joy and great personal satisfaction in solving problems and helping people.

I came to this position still naïve of things worldly, and my eyes were quickly opened. Things like alcoholism, extramarital affairs, cheating, stealing, lying, sluffing off, jealousy, competition, and smoking at work were common everyday occurrences. I was not raised in this culture and quickly found myself resenting the fact that I had not been prepared socially, emotionally, or spiritually to deal with it.

Being of college age, but not in college, I attended the college age Sunday school class at church which was taught by several different individuals, my great aunt, Edna Klietz, being one, and another, a professor at University Wisconsin Whitewater, Dr. Bohi. It was in this class I met young adults my own age who were part of several different on-campus organizations, Campus Crusade for Christ, Intervarsity, and The Navigators. I began attending Bible studies on campus with members of Intervarsity.

Between this Sunday school class and the Bible studies, I gained knowledge of the Bible and how to use it in my everyday life and found support for dealing with the worldliness that surrounded me every day. I was a dried-out sponge soaking in the Springs of Living Water, and it was awesome.

I still lived at home and paid room and board but was able to buy my very first car. It was not a cool sports car, it was a blue Buick LeSabre, four doors, with a 400 HP engine under the hood (her best feature), and she could move when I said go. For the most part, I had the freedom and independence I longed for, but, like I said, I lived at home, and my parents had rules. But let us be clear, I honored some because they made sense, but those that did not make sense, at least to me, not so much. Yes, it was a point of contention, but I did remind my parents I was now an adult.

Like any parent, which being one myself I now understand, my parents just tried to keep me from being hurt, and this was the premise for many of their rules. But keep in mind, it was these very rules that left me unprepared for the worldly things I was now facing. My parents held the thought that if you do not tell them about it, they will not fall into it. Fortunately, I did not fall into it, but once again I credit the protection of the Holy Spirit in me.

I clearly remember telling my parents when they hit me with their justification of "we are doing this for your own good so you will not get hurt," "my life, my mistakes, my consequences, my opportunity to learn." This was just my approach to life. Their advice was not wasted, it rattled around in my head, and, yes, provided guiding light, but to just blindly do what they told me to do because they said so was not my cup of tea. I was going to live it and do it my way, period, and I did.

Flash back…this did not start once I became of age. I embraced this in one form and another at a very young age. By now I had already reaped some of my own consequences, but as one grows older, the stakes become higher. That is just life.

Dating was a part of my life. I was dating a man, a few years older than me, who had already graduated college, worked at a bank, attending my church, and was a grounded Christian. Honestly, it blew me away that he would even give me a second glance, but he did. We did not date all that long, not even a year, but I fell hard, so when he informed me that he was going to Dakar, Senegal, West Africa, for two years as a short-term missionary, and he was breaking up with me, my boat did not just rock, it almost sank.

Here is the thing about dating. My mother, who called me "boy crazy," said if you date someone, it should be the man you are going to marry. It you date a lot of men, you get the reputation of being a loose, easy, wild woman. Furthermore, anyone you date must be a Christian, or you cannot date them. For these reasons, when I had my first date at the age of sixteen, there was a lot of objections.

Now I had been dumped once, in high school, and it hurt. I should have expected it, he was two years ahead of me and, naturally, upon graduation went on to pursue his future. I got over it, eventually. But this time just seemed different; he was older, by five years, wiser, had a job, and was a solid Christian. For sure this was the man God had picked out for me. Not so much. We remained friends, and I was his stateside contact for his newsletter to his supporters, and I hung onto a glimmer of hope, but it did not come to fruition.

Meanwhile, I started dating another guy from work. He was fun, available, had a job, grew up on a farm, and responsible, and we had good times together. Two things nagged at me. First, he would do anything to please me. He just was not the type to stand up to me. If I chose to, I could wrap him around my little finger. Second, he was also a staunch Lutheran who believed he was saved through infant baptism.

The summer I was twenty, I had the opportunity through United World Missions which was affiliated with our church to go on a summer evangelistic missions' trip to Belgium. This was for me, and I immediately began raising support to go. My parents were against it. My mother told me that she was praying that I would not raise the support, and she couldn't understand why people were giving me money.

God answered my prayers. I got all the support I needed. Packed my bags and was off to Chicago O'Hare. My parents drove me to the airport where I met one other girl, the daughter of a missionary.

We flew to New York City JFK International Airport. There we hooked up with Betty Sadler from United World Missions; Joe and Sharon Bobb, leaders of The Navigators at the University of Wisconsin; Whitewater, who I knew through our church; and the rest of the American team.

We spent four weeks in Waremme, Belgium, under the direction of missionary Sam Liebreck doing street evangelism. I had taken seven years of French but was by no means fluent. Using what little knowledge I had, a translation dictionary, and working in groups, we set out working in neighborhoods, parks, a coffee house, and in Sam's church. Our accommodations were in a school. They provided mattresses; we provided our own sleeping bag. We had rows of sinks, separate bathrooms, which consisted of the toilet for guys and girls, and the big shower room across the back lot was on a schedule.

Joining us were additional young people from England, and getting to know them was a treasured experience. We had daily Bible study and prayer time, opportunities for group discussion, and free time to explore the city of Waremme. Our meals were cooked by Belgium women, and we ate and gathered in the mess hall. We all took turns helping out with the serving and clean up. Weekends we went of bus tours and visited Holland, Luxembourg, and Germany.

The full time in Belgium was six weeks, and the very last weekend before returning home was a trip to Paris. I did not go to Paris but instead traveled alone to Dakar, Senegal, West Africa, and spent two weeks at missionary Thelma Wagner's home visiting the man I had dated (who had invited me to come) along with the English School for Missionary kids, the Home of Hope Orphanage, the homes of several other missionaries, and their church.

Belgium was a familiar different, Africa, a real eye opener. This was in 1972 when there was a lot of racial unrest in America. I had an American perspective when I arrived in Africa. I had waist-length very blonde hair, and my skin was white and not tanned at all. It was a bit unnerving to be on the streets of Dakar and have many African people just touch my hair and skin. They were fascinated by my light hair and pale complexion.

African markets sold everything. It was fun to shop, see creative, skilled artist make clothing, jewelry, statues, and more, out of silver, ebony, handwoven clothe, and other local materials. I was able to purchase genuine African handiwork for incredibly reasonable prices. On the other hand, the street markets for fruits, vegetables, meat, fish, and grains were the most unsanitary I had ever witnessed. It was common to see produce freshened by swishing it through water in the gutter and meats covered with flies in the open air. The smells were indescribable. Among the African shoppers were beggars, people with leprosy, and others with the appearance of disease. I experienced firsthand a people and culture I had only heard about from missionaries at church, and there was no comparison.

My transportation was on the back of a scooter, so I was open and exposed. I was shown the typical living situation of many African people. Homes made out of tin and cardboard, and scooting through the neighborhood, I saw rats the size of a small dog. Even in the home where I stayed, I was warned, "Do not just put your feet into your slippers, there may be scorpions. If something falls on your bed, it's just a lizard." Luckily, I never had these experiences, but I did find four- to five-inch cockroaches in the shower. Thelma's home had two showers, and one usually was free of visitors.

The African landscape was as beautiful as it was barren. I saw huge baobab trees, vultures, lizards just roaming, exotic flowers, cliffs above a very blue ocean with sparkling sunshine dancing on the waves. It was here I had my first dip in the Atlantic Ocean which was so clear I could see the bottom. One evening we were invited to an ambassadors' home. Compared to what I had already seen, it was jaw dropping. We also took a smaller boat to visit Gorée Island, just off the coast of Senegal where many African slaves were boarded onto ships to be sold into slavery. Walking around on the island, I saw large lizards, another first of my exotic experiences.

My trip home was from Dakar to New York (beautiful from the air at night) to Chicago where my parents picked me up. Upon my return home, I learned that at the Home of Hope Orphanage, in the kitchen of the missionary's home, where I sat and enjoyed a meal, under the refrigerator that had been behind me, a nest of spitting viper snakes was found. So glad I was spared that experience!

These two months where life-changing. I acquired a totally different perspective of the world. Exposure to a European lifestyle and a less fortunate culture than what we know in America not only gave me a historical perspective, but a greater appreciation for the privilege of being born and living in the United States. In and of itself, this was a journey, a new beginning, a fresh start. Not so much in what I did, but in who I was and how I viewed the world around me. God had purpose in this adventure for me. One question that had nagged me for many years was that of becoming a missionary. This grew out of the many missionary conferences that were held at our church. I had told God many times, "If you want me to I will, but please God, not Africa!" God told me, "Been there, done that. I have other plans for you." Praise the Lord!

I returned to work at Nasco but soon changed jobs, leaving customer service and becoming the switchboard operator and facility receptionist while also doing work for some of the company executives. I love the new challenge and perspective this position afforded me.

I no longer dated the fellow from work; he actually dumped me. Now, single and unattached, I embraced a new perspective about men. I had been dumped three times, and I was done with that. From now if I chose to date, it would be only for fun and they could pay the tab, and should one dare to get serious, I was going to be the dumper. I was actually looking forward to the opportunity. I was giving myself a good ten years before considering a serious relationship. My goal was to move out of my parents' home and get a place of my own, so I started some serious saving of my money.

Two things stand out about my time as the receptionist at Nasco. Talking was my job, a voice was necessary. This was during a time when smoking was allowed in the office, at your desk. I would look down the hall across the top of the partitions and there was a perpetual cloud of smoke. I was allergic to cigarette smoke and continually lost my voice to laryngitis. I learned to squeak like an expert and kept bottles of cough syrup in my drawer.

I also had my first life-threatening emergency experience, and it was up to me to be point person for calling for help and directing traffic. One of our executives who I could see in his office from my desk had a heart attack. I saw the onset, made the calls, and did exactly what needed to be done. I did not save his life, but my role was crucial to him receiving the help he needed. I had no particular training, but I instinctively knew what to do and stayed calm and in charge. Do not tell me this was not a God thing!

One thing to note before moving on. It was New Year's Eve, 1973, and God gave me a very specific message. "Pray for the man you are going to marry." Puzzled, I said ok, but marriage is not on my radar for at least another ten years.

I did some significant stretching and growing during these few years of school free independence, and God was right there guiding, protecting, and preparing me for my next, fresh start, and new beginning.

For we are God's handiwork, created in Christ Jesus to do good works, which God prepared in advance for us to do. (Ephesians 2:10 NLT)

Point to be taken here, "which God prepared in advance for us (specifically me) to do."

CHAPTER 9

Love

Perspective: love. I traded off my blue Buick LeSabre and bought myself a bright red, hatch back, bucket seats, automatic on the floor, Javelin. It maybe was not the hottest, fastest ride in town, but it sure beat my four-door sedan. I was movin' and groovin' now!

Just before my trip to Belgium, my sister got married and lived in an apartment in town. It was fun having a place to go and just hang out with her that was not under the watchful eye of my parents. Though they seemed to have loosened up a bit, they still were parents. Living at home limits one's privacy, and unfortunately, I could not yet afford to move out. One makes the best of what you have. It was nice to have the occasional opportunities to do stuff with my sister and her husband.

In our town we had what was called "the circuit." Basically, just a route through main street, around a block on each end, and driving "the circuit" was the thing to do. There was the municipal lot where guys would park and talk and just hang out. A simple pleasure until some had to ruin it by selling drugs there. The municipal lot got a new name, "the pot lot," and it was now patrolled by police, and you could no longer park there.

I had gone out a couple of times with another girl from work, and we just had pizza, drove the circuit, and called it a night. She had pointed out this one guy who drove a dark green Chevelle that she thought was interesting. It really was of no consequence to me. I was into just having a good time, not dating.

I frequently drove the circuit just for something to do but honestly did not really know anyone in particular out there. Just put the radio on, drove around, and then headed home, where I secluded myself in my little ten by twelve room. I did not hang out with my parents much, and looking back, that saddens me, but it was what it was when I was twenty-two.

Along about the end of March, I noticed that green Chevelle seeming to follow me. It would even follow me home some nights. At this point in my life, I had to park across the alley in my great uncle's driveway because my dad was not about to have to move my car every morning to go to work. He left slightly earlier than me. I remember sitting in my car and waiting until the Chevelle was on the other side of the block and then running across the lawn into the house. I really did not know who this person was, and it felt a little like being stalked. With lights out I would look out the window, and after one drive by, it was gone. This went on for a little over a month, but near the end of April, the car changed. Now it was a lime green and black, Z28 Camaro, and it made noise. Guess whose interest was sparked now!

One Saturday I was out washing my car, and the Camaro pulled up. I kind of knew who he was by asking around. He was a preacher's son, and he worked for the same company my dad worked at. He says to me, "Ask your dad if he wants some pine trees, I have some to get rid of." He drove off. I did not ask, it was odd.

Friday night, May 3, 1974. I went with my sister and her husband to the local Home Show that was held in the municipal building. At the end of the last aisle, I spotted the guy who drove the Camaro. Cowboy boots, tight blue jeans, leather jacket, longish side burns, blondish hair. He said, "Hi," and I said, "Hi."

I left with my sister, got into my car, and hit the circuit. Was not long before I picked up a tail, the lime green Z28 Camaro. I decided to see how far I could push this, so I went home, ran into the house to get some gum, and by the time I came out, the Camaro was in my driveway. Score!

His name was David, and he asked me if I would like a ride in his car. Dah! Yes! But I curbed my enthusiasm and said, "Sure," and just let me move my car.

We drove the circuit, and around town, out and about. Nice car, great ride. We talked the entire time, and he brought me home at 1:00 am. This was the only night he ever kept me out beyond midnight. For future reference, my parents loved this one fact about him.

Remember me saying I was going to be the dumper the next time? God had a different plan.

David asked me out Saturday night to the car races in Oregon. We went with a good friend of his and his wife, and both drove their own cars, but his friend had a white Z28 Camaro just like David's. It was a bit nippy that night, and we wrapped up together in his leather jacket to keep warm. Went out of pizza afterward. Was home before midnight, and I got my first kiss in the car, in the driveway before he walked me to the door.

David was persistent. The following weeks, every day, he called me before I left for work. Called me at break time, called me when I ran home for lunch, called me at afternoon break time, called me when I got home, and showed up at the door around 5:30. We would hang out until 10:00 when he had me home, and he would call me once more before turning in for the night. We went out every Friday and Saturday night and just hung out on Sunday afternoons.

We were not into anything fancy or big expensive dates. A burger, a movie, ride the circuit, and take drives on Sunday afternoon. We talked a lot but sometimes just enjoyed the quiet of each other's company. Memorial weekend we went to his friends' home and listen to the Indy 500 and had a cook out.

Unknown to us, our parents met at the Friday night fish fry at the Legion Dugout. David's mom informed my mom that this relationship was serious. My mom did not think so and asked why she thought so. Her answer, "I can tell by the way David says her name."

It was mid-June; the weather was nice and we decided to take a Friday off work. David had to do something with his car, and then we were going to go to the Brookfield Zoo. Prior to this week, I told my mom, "I think David is going to ask me to marry him, what do I do?" Understand, I am twenty-two years old, and all my life, my mother was telling me what to do and how to do it. Her answer at this most opportune moment in my life, "I don't know, you will have to decide that for yourself!" Knock me out cold! Really!

Since my mother was zero help, I went straight to God and asked Him the exact same question. God had one answer, and one only, and it was a question. "Is he saved?"

Honestly, I didn't know. One cannot assume that just because he was a preacher's kid he was, but in my heart, I knew this was critical, make or break, and God wanted me to find out. Ok then, Father, here is what I am asking for, I lay my fleece before you. I don't know if putting out a fleece for God is the appropriate thing to do, but I did it. "If you want me to marry David, then I need to know two things: (1) he has asked Jesus into his heart, and (2) he remembers where and when he did it."

Historically for me asking a direct question like this would unnerve me, but I had total peace. We were on the front porch, just the two of us, and I asked David if he had asked Jesus into his heart. Not skipping a beat, he said "yes." I asked him if he remembered when he did it, and not only did he remember when, but where and who it was that prayed with him. Huh…Guess God gave me His answer, and at least now I was prepared should the subject arise.

It was a beautiful Friday. We had a great time at the zoo. We were out on the highway just driving along, and David says to me, "Do you think you would consider marrying me?" I said, "Sure." It was a done deal. Sounds simple and dull, but the atmosphere was electric. We went to a jewelry store at a mall and looked at rings; he wanted an idea of what I liked. On the drive home, we planned the whole wedding and what we each liked and wanted. Back in town we stopped at the filling station where David worked, and he told his boss the news. This was Friday, June 15, 1974.

Monday, June 18, David picked me up at work for lunch, and we went to our favorite burger stand, Jimbos, and parked under the big tree in front. David got our food, and back in the car, he told me to look in the console. I opened it and looked inside. There was a small box. He told me to take it out and open it. It was a beautiful diamond engagement ring, circled by smaller diamonds. I returned to work, officially engaged.

We had only been dating six weeks, and honestly, for me, it felt different. Three times I had fallen hard, but not this time. I thoroughly enjoyed being with David, and he made my heart skip a beat. Perhaps I entered into this relationship with guarded caution over my heart. Face it, getting dumped hurt, and I had no desire to go there again. Assuredly, this was different, it was right, and it was good. I didn't realize it then, but falling "in love" with David was to be a lifelong process. What a journey it has been.

Back to Monday, June 18. My dad's birthday was June 18, so I got engaged on my dad's birthday. Mom had invited the kids' home for a birthday dinner, and David of course was included. When David arrived, we went out to the front porch where my dad was sitting in his chair reading the newspaper. I said, "Dad, I have a birthday present for you." I held my left hand over the newspaper and said, "a future son-in-law." Without hesitation my dad says, "Oh that old thing, it's out of a Cracker Jack Box." Welcome to the family David! My mother was mortified and promptly scolded my dad with her infamous "Oh Melvin!"

David and I could have gotten married before fall. We knew what we wanted, how we wanted it, and the sooner the better. My parents on the other hand had a different view of things and said they needed at least a year to save money to pay for a wedding. Since May 3, the date of our first date, fell on a Saturday in 1975, it became our wedding date. In the process of planning the wedding, my mother and I argued for almost the entire year over the punch. We knew what we wanted, but she insisted that was not "punch." In the end, she got her way, with just a little compromise.

Soon after our engagement, I changed jobs and started working as the receptionist, proofreader, and doing odd jobs for executives at the local newspaper, *The Daily Union*, but also put out a Dairy magazine, *Hoard's Dairyman*. David's job took him out of town for one whole week to do an equipment installation. Every day of that one week, a bouquet of flowers was delivered to me at work. We all worked in one big room, so when the flowers were brought in, everyone watched with great anticipation to see who they were for. Five days in a row, they came to me, and each day, they got a little bigger. This was just the beginning of the many wonderful ways I have been shown love.

(To note: In March, as I drove by, David said to a friend; "see the girl in that red car, I am going to marry her".)

CHAPTER 10

Commitment

Perspective: commitment. Our year of engagement was spent getting to know each other, meeting each other's families and extended families, making plans, and figuring out where we would live and what we would need to set up a home.

On a whim David and I decided to give each other an engagement present. His name was "Apple Blossom," and he was the cutest "little" bundle of fur, a St. Bernard puppy. Between the two of us, we housed Apple at our parent's homes. As cute as this "little" bundle of fur was, he definitely got bigger.

Each of our homes would have a special memory, and so it was with our first home where we started life together. It was the bringing together of our pieces and parts and mixing them with our new pieces and parts, the journey from "yours and mine" to "ours."

A man from David's father's church owned a home just a few blocks from my parents and my sister. The rent was reasonable, so after the first of the year, we started renting it and David moved in with a few possessions. There was work to be done in this house, and our landlord gave us free reign to do what we wanted. The basement was an awful mess from previous renters. Dog poo was everywhere. The landlord took care of cleaning that up. It was a creepy old basement with an old cistern area the older homes use to have and a big dirty old oil furnace. I visited this basement twice.

The kitchen left much to be desired, so the landlord said we were free to put in new cabinets, counter, and sink, and he would pay for it. My sister's husband happened to be a cabinet maker, so we had him do the job. In the process of cleaning out the old, we discovered a significant leak from the roof. Once again, the land-lord fixed the roof and made things dry and secure.

After we had thoroughly cleaned the house, and I mean dis-infecting it, we set about painting the walls. To say the least, it was colorful. An array of yellow, orange, blue, green, and lime green, pink, and lavender filled our color palette. One room had been painted black, and we found some holes in the plaster that had been covered with black electrical tape. We patched, painted, and wall-papered, learning new skills along the way. We decided a wood burning stove would keep us cozy and add atmosphere, so this too was installed.

Furniture and appliances were next. As a wedding gift, David's parents gave us a washer and dryer which fit perfectly in the kitchen. They also had an old kitchen table and chairs that they passed down to us, along with a used futon. My grandmother had a really nice old dining room table in her granary that she gave us. David took on the job of stripping and refinishing it and the four leaves that went with it. Our parents both gave us the bedroom sets we had in our rooms at home, along with springs and mattresses. All that was left was a stove, refrigerator, sofa, and chair which we purchased. Through connections we secured a couple of area carpets which partially covered the not-so-great wooden floors. Curtains and a couple of light fixtures and the house became our first home.

Come spring there were bridal showers, and we received won-derful gifts that help filled the cupboards, pantry, and the linen closet. We were feeling accomplished and prepared.

We also learned a few things about getting along with each other. The work at the house, while both still working full time, wore us out and shortened our fuses. We had a couple of arguments and exhibitions of frustration and shedding of tears. But this was good. Life is not meeting, falling in love, and riding off into the sunset into perfect bliss. This was never my take on life, but then again, other than my sister and parents, I had not experienced such differences of opinions and the subsequent reactions. One big difference, your parents and sister will always be your parents and sister; it is a birth thing. But David and I, together, that was a choice. The stakes were higher.

Before our wedding, we needed to accomplish one more thing. Apple was not really a house dog. He liked being inside with us enough, but he really loved the outdoors. It suited him. Needless to say, he also needed good shelter and secure confinement. David took care of both, building a large dog house and erecting a chain link fence. For the wedding and honeymoon, we boarded Apple out.

The weekend of our wedding arrived. There was the rehearsal, the dinner, and then the day of the wedding. We had planned a 6:00 pm wedding that had a little southern flavor to it, and David wore tux with tails. My sister, an excellent seamstress, sewed the four bridesmaid dresses and the flower girl's dress. Everything came together. We got our hair done, the cake, flowers (yellow roses), and food arrived for the reception in the church basement. Dressed and ready to go, the photographer captured some "light was perfect" shots that caused me to be late, heading down the aisle. This made David, who is never late for anything, slightly anxious.

We had four attendants, ring bearer, and flower girl. Two soloists, my aunt and uncle, and two pastors, my church pastor, and David's dad. A lot of thought went into our service, and it was important that the message of salvation was given. We had a candle lighting as part of our service in which we had to blow out our individual candles. I still had my veil over my face when I started blowing, sending the veil floating straight for the flame. I stopped just in time, thinking I could shake the flame out. This only sprayed wax around. David took the candle and blew it out. Shortly before 7:00 pm, we were pronounced husband and wife.

The reception line was never ending. Between the two of us, we had over 400 guests. This made for a very crowded reception dinner in the basement. Back then it was the custom to take pictures after the wedding. The process was time consuming and some guests had already left by the time we made it to dinner.

Then there was the driving around town and the honking of horns while dragging tin cans behind the car. Sadly, though wisely, David had made the decision that he should sell his Camaro before we were married. Having one car that was paid for just made financial sense, so my Javelin was our chariot for the wedding ride. It had developed a temperamental driver's door choosing at random times to fly open, and so it did. Fortunately for the honeymoon, it behaved itself.

We set off for our honeymoon, which David had arranged by himself and kept it a surprise for me. We had a bridal suite at the Clock Tower Inn in Rockford, Illinois, for our wedding night and the next day headed to northern Wisconsin where he had rented a cottage at a resort on St. Germain lake. We had to purchase a few groceries, stopped at a bakery, and then settled in. The bed was a three-quarter size bed, very cozy. I had dreams about Apple every night. The oven was a gas oven, on which I had no experience. First time I turned the burner on I almost set myself on fire as I cranked it wide open, fast.

Our first day David decided we would go for a canoe ride on the lake. I did not know how to swim, and David was not a seasoned swimmer. Neither of us had ever rowed a canoe before. We wore life jackets. Heading out was not bad until a wind picked up. It turned out to be that I was more of a hinderance than a help, so David rowed alone, getting us safely back to shore, but he was worn out. The next day we decided to stay on land and found a hiking path through the woods. It was beautiful, but as we traversed the path, a snake wiggled up and snapped out at David catching his boot, which it did not penetrate. We hopped up onto a rock and, once we felt safe, walked swiftly back to the car.

Third day out we decided to go for a ride to Bond Falls in Michigan. It was a beautiful setting with a bridge that went across the falls. There was still some snow on the ground, adding to the ambiance. We decided that I should take a picture of David standing on the rocks in the water fall. He made it out there ok, I snapped the picture, and he slipped and fell. It was cold and wet, and we headed for the cabin, heater going. Fourth day was going to be a car only adventure, doing what we loved to do, exploring. It was great until Highway B turned into gravel. It was still wet from melting snow in northern Wisconsin, and we decided it would be better to turn around and go a different direction. In doing so, we found ourselves stuck on the side of the road where the ground was softer, muddier, and not user-friendly. David got out, gave me direction, and he pushed. We succeeded in digging the car deeper, up to the axels, in mud.

Mind you, we are literally in the middle of nowhere. No houses, no people, just unending northern woods. No cell phones back then either. Our only choice was to walk to the main road and hope someone drove by. My knight in shining armor gave me all the money and told me to put it in my bra, you know, in case we run into some not so nice people, and then he instructed me that should we see a bear, I should run and climb up the first tree I saw. This was a romantic reality check for this new bride.

We walked three miles to the main highway, incident free. A car happened by, and they stopped. It was a couple from Canada. We told them our plight, and they generously offered to give us a ride to the nearest town for help, seventeen miles down the road. They dropped us at a filing station and wished us well. A wonderful man with a tow truck, drove us back to our car, pulled us out of the mud, advised us to stick to main highways this time of year, and was on his way after we paid him. That night David slept on the couch because his back really hurt.

We spent the last day of our honeymoon, in the cabin, playing strip poker by the fireplace. We had intended to stay for two weeks, but early Saturday morning we packed up and headed home. We picked up Apple who was so happy to see us and went to spend our first night in our home.

On Sunday we had our first entertaining of guest as family members came for lunch and joined us in the opening of wedding gifts. Fortunately, meal preparation was easy; there were many leftovers from the reception.

For better, for worse, in sickness and in health, until death we do part. The vow we took and pledged to each other before God and these people. For me, I was free from my parental home, and I had a home of my own. Together, we acquired our independence, to become one in God, dependent on each other, and on God, to form a new home, a new family, a new beginning, and start a new journey.

…That is why a man leaves his father and mother and is united to his wife, and they become one flesh. (Genesis 2:24 NIV)

CHAPTER 11

Family

Perspective: family. Early summer we heard about a housing development program through the government program FmHA. We applied and qualified for the program. Together with four other families, we set out to build five homes. Our sweat equity would be our downpayment. The projects began in the fall and continued through to the next July. Our project had a supervisor who guided us through the hows, dos and don'ts of construction. We provided what tools we had and the rest was furnished by the FmHA program. Concrete, plumbing, and electrical were all done by licensed professionals. Basic building materials were purchased for us, but we were able to choose from a limited selection, cupboards, counters, stains, paint colors (our palette became one color this time), and carpet. We acquired knowledge and skills that we would use again in the future.

The end of October I became pregnant, and by Christmas, morning sickness had settled in for a three-month visit. This was to be the first grandchild on both sides of our family, and we wanted to tell the parents together. We conjured up a plan to get them all to come to our house on short notice. We had a plumbing problem and had water all over and needed help and supplies to clean up.

On key our parents showed up, dressed in old clothes and bearing enough supplies to do the job. Upon their arrival, clearly, they noticed that there was no imminent crisis, and puzzled, we asked them to sit down. David shared the wonderful news, and there was joy all around.

Anticipating parenthood was clearly a huge new beginning. In preparation we took childbirth classes at the hospital with multiple other couples. Upon finishing we were sent home to practicing our breathing and coaching skills. The class also included a tour of the maternity ward and films on what to expect. It was very educational and helpful to the point we felt prepared.

We moved into our new home just two weeks before our baby was born. Through showers and contacts with friends, we were able to set up a nursery with everything our baby would need. David continued to work his full-time job and his part-time job at the filing station some nights and weekends. I had stopped working when the bouts of morning sickness went into full swing.

Being educated and informed about pregnancy and child birth is one thing. Actually, going through it, quite another. I had gained fifty pounds; my shoe size went from a 5 ½ to a 7. It was hot, and we only had a window air conditioner for our bedroom. My bags were packed, and on August 6, I went into labor.

Around 7 am the next morning, August 7, our 7 Lb. 1 oz., 19 ½ inch-long daughter made her debut, and life for us forever changed. While we were still dating, we had talked about children and names, so even before we were married, our first child, which I was certain had to be a girl, had a name—Amiee Joy, meaning "beloved joy."

We still had Apple, and he became a protector, keeping a close eye on this new member of the family. Our new home did not have a lawn so when we happened on a great price for sod that was coming close to the end of its season, we purchased, hauled, and laid enough to cover the front and one side of the house. The back was a sloping hill and grass seed had been laid. Looking to have a natural boundary in the back, we planted over a hundred small bush-like trees and, in front, a bed of tulip bulbs for that burst of color in the spring. We held a baby dedication dinner for all the family and sponsors, and time flew to our first Christmas as a family of three. Amiee was chosen to be the live baby in the Christmas program nativity scene, and she did an awesome job of laying still and being quiet.

Special memories of our second home began with the fact that we built it! A major accomplishment in and of itself. But this home welcomed our first child, a gift from God. On the funnier side, Apple managed to get out of his kennel in pursuit of a female in heat two miles away. Somehow mice got into our basement and made a nest in the wedding gift paper I had saved. Where was the camera when David was in the backyard with his cowboy boots and shorts stomping on mice as they escaped from a bag? Then there was our midnight ride when, after a visit to the emergency room because Amiee would not stop crying. Nothing found to be wrong, and as he handed our wailer back to us, the doctor told us to just take her for a ride until she settles down. Two hours later, we were back home with a sleeping child.

A change in jobs and location prompted our third move, first from home to our first house, second to the house we built, and now to a duplex about a half hour away in Janesville. Amiee was eighteen months old. We moved into this new home on New Year's Eve day, and by morning, a huge snow storm had us snowed in. But all our stuff was safely inside, and I had done quick work of settling in. We were not able to keep Apple with us, so a friend offered to take him, but by the following summer, he was not doing good and had to be put down. It was sad, but it was life.

While living in our third home, I had to learn to navigate my way around a much larger city than I was accustom to. David drew me color-coded maps. Once I set out on my bicycle and my tire started going flat. I stopped in a filling station to put air into the tire and promptly blew it up. The bang was deafening, and David had to pack up Amiee and come rescue me. It was in this home that our sweet little girl became a shop lifter, not once, but twice. She had her dad's heart wrapped around her little finger, and he purchased the big bunny and the ball she had lifted from the shelf. I also experienced the pains of morning sickness, the flu, and food poisoning all in a matter of five days, loosing seven pounds, not recommended for a weight loss program.

As stated, I became pregnant again, David had changed jobs, and we found ourselves packing up and moving back to our home town of Fort Atkinson, for our fourth move. Amiee was two plus years old. We were lucky to rent the home of friends who had to move out of state for his job for an undetermined amount of time. Their home was in the country, near my aunt and uncle's farm and my grandma's farm. The home was large, a ranch, and had an above-ground pool. I was already dealing with morning sickness which made this move challenging. We settled in and life was good. David picked up his part-time job at the filling station again.

Each home has its own special memories. This time it was the winter of 1978–1979 and we were hit with one of the worst snow storms in our area. The driveway was long, we did not have a snow blower, and after shoveling for seven hours, David made it to the end of the driveway where he was greeted by a seven plus foot bank of snow. We gave a call to my cousin who lived nearby and had a front-end loader on his tractor. He graciously came and dug us out. David and Amiee made cut out cookies for Christmas. I stayed out of the kitchen until they were done. The deal was, they would bake, I would clean up. They got the best end of that deal. This home was to welcome our son, and we would watch the start of sibling dynamics take shape.

By the last three months of this pregnancy, I was dealing with morning sickness again. My weight gains this time was only twenty pounds. David's brother was getting married on June 9, and I was past my due date. David was to be in the wedding, but they moved him to usher and asked that I sit at the back of the church. I went into labor the evening of June 10. We packed Amiee up and took her to my mother and headed for the hospital. By the next morning, June 11, our son was born. We had already picked his name out shortly after Amiee was born, he was Austin Ryan, meaning great gift of God. We felt incredibly blessed.

Before Austin was two, we had once again packed up and made our fifth move to the other side of that country block as the family we were renting from were returning home. This home was owned by my uncle's brother, and just down the road, good friends lived. It had a big yard and a woods at the top of the hill that we could explore. Our time in this home was marked by some ups and downs.

My sister and her husband, due to a job change for him, moved to North Carolina. This was not how I thought life was going to be, and as much as it saddened me, it seemed to upset my parents more. David lost his job so for a time we switched roles. He was the stay-at-home dad, and I went back to work. David did find another job, and I quit working to come home and be mom and homemaker again. Taking our children to a babysitter simply was not an option for us. During our time here, Amiee started kindergarten.

Most eye opening was David having a TIA, mini stroke which put him in the hospital for ten days for complete rest. Turns out it was caused by high blood pressure. He was only thirty. During those ten days, I faced the real possibility of losing David and becoming a single parent, at worst, or possibly having a husband who would need to be cared for.

God is good, all the time! His grace is always sufficient, His love beyond comprehension, His peace unexplainable, and His mercy the greatest blessing.

"For I know the plans I have for you," says the LORD, "they are plans for good and not for disaster, to give you a future and a hope." (Jeremiah 29:11 NLT)

The worst scenario was never realized, not even close. With medication, and a period of adjustment, David's blood pressure was controlled, and no damage was done. I did however live with this possibility in the back of my mind, and consciously or not, I strove to make myself prepared should that day ever come.

When you are young and you have all of life yet to live, your focus is occupied by caring for children, home, jobs, health, provision, and survival of life while trying to squeeze in some fun moments and memories. You are not even considering "what ifs." This was a wake-up call, and one I have learned to be eternally grateful for. What David and I had together was never to be taken for granted. The moments of every single day are a precious gift from God; do not waste or misuse them. This would forever shape my view and perspective of our life together.

Did not know it at this time, but this was just the first of three serious TIAs and other health issues David would have.

In addition to David's significant health event and my sister moving, and our temporary role change, more memories were made while living here. While helping my cousin on his barn roof, David slipped and fell off onto the concrete cow yard. Fortunately, he was only cold, smelly, and bruised, nothing broken.

We had two mobile children in this home. Amiee and Austin got their first swing set, lending to hours of play for them. Austin wiggled his way into a lilac bush, and the only way we could free him was to saw a branch off. A catalpa tree in the backyard grew these long bean pods. Unknown to us, Austin chose to snack on them, and we only realized what he had done when the evidence appeared in the diaper. Thank goodness they did not harm him. Amiee discovered the telephone and was quick to engage in her first live conversations. Artists that our children were, they decided that taking crayons to the wall was the best form of expression. A bat came to visit early one morning, flying and diving at us. Luckily the kids were upstairs, and it was contained to the main floor where David eventually captured and released it. We had a very large garden and a raspberry patch, both which yielded a great store of food for our freezer. We enjoyed many family hikes into the woods behind our house and our kids got their first real taste of nature.

CHAPTER 12

Growing Up

Perspective: growing up. As children should, ours did, they grew up. Before Amiee finished kindergarten, we moved for the sixth time, back into town, just a block from my parents. With a child now in school, we felt the need for some permanence, roots. This home held memories of its own for us also. There was the snake in the yard, found by Amiee as she was pulling Austin in a wagon. From her screams we fully expected to see a lot of blood as she, leaving her brother behind, ran for the house. Another bat came to visit while we lived here. The kids were upstairs in bed, and David was in the shower. I was downstairs when it started to swoop. I crawled under the dining room table and started yelling for David to come. He did not hear me, but Amiee did and ran to the bathroom and said, "Daddy, someone is killing momma downstairs." Grabbing just a bath towel, he came to my rescue, catching the bat in his towel. I was so consumed with instructing him to get it outside that I hardly heard him tell me he needed a pair of pants.

Our first experience decorating cutout Christmas cookies at the kitchen table with both kids was memorable. Frosting, colored sugar, and sprinkles were everywhere, but so were the giggles, smiles, and laughter. More amusement came as birds ate fermented mulberries from the tree in the front yard and literally staggered as they walked. It was here that I got my first (and last) flu vaccination, and not so amusing was how sick I got from it. It was worse than the time I had morning sickness and food poison with the flu and even child birth.

Because we were renting this home, we again looked into a government home finance program and qualified. We found a home, on the same street, just at the other end, about three blocks from my parents. The home qualified for the loan, and we moved for the seventh time. Amiee was in first grade, and Austin was three. We would live in this home until after both children had graduated college and married.

Many are the cherished memories this home holds in our hearts. Twice we painted the exterior, once it was done by some men who were teachers during the school year, and painters over the summer. One was a neighbor from my childhood, one was my science teacher in middle school, and my driver's education teacher in high school, and both our children had him in middle school. The second time we painted ,we did it ourselves. Huge, but rewarding task once we were done.

We remodeled the upstairs which was a half bath and two bedrooms which needed some closets, doors, drywall, paint, and carpet. The stairway leading up there was modified and carpeted also. The walls in the remainder of the home received several different colored coats of paint over the years and the kitchen cupboards as well.

Crochet and cross-stitch were my pastime hobbies, and during our time in this home I crocheted curtains for the living room, the dining area bay window, and kitchen windows. I cross-stitched pictures from patterns I drew for all of the walls in the living room and our bedroom and stenciled the kitchen walls.

I enjoyed all things old and incorporated many treasures into our home. I loved Christmas and fell naturally into collecting Santa figures of all types and angels, which too became part of our year-round décor. Geese also caught my heart and were prominent in the kitchen.

During our years here, the theme of our Christmas tree changed three times. Changing from the original variety sort of ornaments, I spent about four months making, by hand, satin poinsettias. Six to eight inches in diameter and forty-six to be sure. As the angels and Santa started taking over, I created ornaments to reflect this theme, using a variety of materials and crocheting. We had live Christmas trees the entire time we lived here, and searching for the best one was a family adventure.

This home was not large, a four-bedroom cape cod, one and half baths, and a partially finished basement. It had a one car-detached garage which was plenty until I returned to work and the kids started driving. I was the lucky one to get the garage.

The yard needed work, and to live up to dad's expectations, I worked hard at it, but David really invested his time and talents. He built a square-foot garden in which we raised strawberries, herbs, and vegetables. David also planted apple trees, a cherry tree, and one really awesome peach tree that bore the biggest and sweetest peaches ever. We also had a small raspberry patch which yielded well. In fourth grade Austin brought home a pine tree for Arbor Day which made it into our yard also, to this day is still there and very tall. A lilac bush and some flower beds rounded off the landscaping, with some space left over for a nice green lawn. There when we moved in was a silver maple tree that shaded the one side of the home and was full and beautiful, providing plenty of exercise when it decided to drop its leaves. We had a small space for a patio perfect for outdoor meals and a chimenea for warm fires. To make room to park an extra car, we expanded the driveway and had to, at one time, replace some sidewalk raised by tree roots. Two large trees came down on the terraces, one because of disease and one because of wind during a storm.

While living here, we replaced our living room furniture three times, our kitchen appliances, and washer and dryer once. We had a pipe burst once and did battle with some mold in the bathroom. Some big old bumble bees made their home in the attic and found their way down to pay us a visit. The exterminator paid them a visit, and we plugged their point of entry. An oil burning furnace was removed and replaced with gas, and central air was put in. Both helped the home stay comfortable. New storm windows were installed upstairs, and the electrical was upgraded from 110 to 220.

I experienced a lot of different emotions about this home. What started out critical of all its flaws grew into comfort of its character, appreciation for its shelter, enjoyment of its peace, and satisfaction with its location. Its quirks were eclectic, giving it artful style, independence, and a personality all its own.

A house became a shelter, retreat, security, belonging, and home—our home.

It was in this home that God dealt with an attitude I harbored in the back of my mind. It had not always been there, and I did not enter into marriage with it. We had been married a number of years before it started festering. Looking back, it was clearly Satan attempting to tear apart what God had put together—our home and marriage.

I hate what I am about to confess. This should never have even come onto my radar, but sadly, it did. Being newlywed, starting a family, with job changes and moves, was exciting, inspiring, and an adventure. But mixed into all these changes is the reality that God brought two strangers together, who, despite the love they had for each other, had to learn more about each other than just your "likenesses," and "differences," but how to establish the middle ground of compromise and respect. You both have different visions of what that should look like and how it should be accomplished.

The perspective I have at this writing is so different from what it was back in the earlier years of our marriage. Simply put, I had a lot to learn; we both did. Remember my seventh-grade homeroom teacher, Mr. Wildermuth? He told my parents that their daughter, me, was strong willed and independently minded. He was right. More than my parents, I had to learn how to manage these gifts, and yes, I mean gifts that God blessed me with.

David and I did not always see eye to eye. Imagine that! We even had different paths to obtaining solutions. Not unheard of. I also mentioned that with me, what you see is what you get. I could be a stuffer, but generally, I was a knee jerk reactor. These still remain though, through years of practice, are managed. As such, back in the day, when I got frustrated, I would yell, but my favorite was to slam doors. I quickly outgrew the yelling and door slamming, moving on to over analyzing everything, not a healthy habit to nurture. Analyzing became conversations, and my timing was bad. David was a morning person, while I was a night owl, and we still are. When he was ready sleep, I was ready to talk. This is not the way to communicate in a marriage.

But here is the thing. I allowed Satan to plant a thought in my head. Did not realize it at the time, but there it was. That thought? *Well, if this doesn't work out, I will just get a divorce. After all, my dad had been married and divorced before he met my mom, so if he could, I can too.*

I want to be up front right here. My dad did not receive Jesus as his Lord and Savior until after he had married my mom. It was an Easter Sunday, and his life was dramatically changed. I did not know him before this as it happened before I was born.

Deep down I knew better. God gave David to me and me to him, a clear, undeniable fact. I was never proactive about this deep dark thought, but the fact that it even existed was wrong. In addition, I apparently thought it was up to me to change David and make him into the person I thought he should be. Sadly, I did engage in this endeavor. We would be much happier, right? Wrong! For the record, my efforts failed, and that was a good thing. Had they not, Satan would have won. But God was ultimately in charge, and once again, His protection was over us.

One thing I always did for as long as I can remember was daily reading my Bible and praying. This was instilled in me at a very young age by my parents. This one morning God had me in Ephesians, specifically chapter five, the first part instruction on living the Christian life, but emphatically for me, verses 21–33:

> And further, submit to one another out of reverence for Christ. For wives, this means submit to your husbands as to the Lord. For a husband is the head of his wife as Christ is the head of the church. He is the Savior of his body, the church. As the church submits to Christ, so you wives should submit to your husbands in everything.
>
> For husbands, this means love your wives, just as Christ loved the church. He gave up his life for her to make her holy and clean, washed by the cleansing of God's word. He did this to present her to himself as a glorious church without a spot or wrinkle or any other blemish. Instead, she will be holy and without fault. In the same way, husband's ought to love their wives as they love their own bodies. For a man who loves his wife actually shows love for himself. No one hates his own body but feeds and cares for it, just as Christ cares for the church. And we are members of his body. As the Scriptures say, "A man leaves his father and mother and is joined to his wife, and the two are united into one." This is a great mystery, but it is an illustration of the way Christ and the church are one. So again, I say, each man must love his wife as he loves himself, and the wife must respect her husband. (Ephesians 5:21–33 NLT)

God spoke to my heart that day and in no uncertain terms said to me, "Carol, divorce is not an option. You will stop trying to change David, it is not your place to do so. I gave David to you. From now on, you will respect him as the head of your home, you will love him unconditionally, and receive him just as he is. Pray for him."

I listened, I did what God told me, and this has been one of the most life-changing choices I have ever made. I did a 180 that day, and I never looked back. God said so; I obeyed, and I cannot even begin to measure the blessings I personally have received for this one act of obedience.

In the years of our marriage, time and again, even to this day, God has shown me how perfect His choice of David for me is. Honoring God in your marriage relationship is the single most fulfilling blessing, second to your relationship with Jesus, that you will ever experience. God knows me better than I know myself. He not only has supplied needs I didn't know I had, He has provided an abundance of wants that I didn't realize I wanted. Peace, contentment, fulfillment, satisfaction, grace, mercy, joy, and love, only begin to describe how my cup overflows, every day!

CHAPTER 13

Parenting

Perspective: parenting. My mother often said, "Once a parent, always a parent." When my children were small, I questioned the validity of this statement. Surely once they became adults and moved out, parenting job was done. Time has proven, mom was right, I was wrong.

Transitioning from single, just married, to parenthood is like a 180-degree turn in lifestyle. Just being an adult requires responsibility, but being a parent shoots the responsibility factor right off the Richter scale. You come home with this beautiful baby in your arms, and the next thing you know you are buried in laundry, dirty diapers (we started out with cloth diapers, I know, unheard of today), formula (prep, feeding, and clean up after projectile eruption because baby ate too fast), baby food, car seats, high chairs, strollers, and everything else it takes to make the baby comfortable, warm, safe, and happy. Just wait until the first time they get sick and cannot tell you what is wrong!

You thought you were tired when you stayed out late on a date and had to go to work the next morning. That was nothing compared to feedings every two to three hours, 24/7, not to mention the extra half hour or so it took for the baby to burp, change the diaper, and settle back down to sleep. Just about the time you fall back asleep, it starts all over again. You do not realize it when in the thick of things, especially the first time, but this really does not last forever, and by the time you bring the second beautiful baby home, you have an established routine and game plan.

Unless there are special circumstances, the second one truly is easier.

From my perspective of retirement, those truly were the "easy" days.

Oh, how you looked forward to sitting, crawling, standing, teeth, solid food, walking, toilet trained, and ability to amuse one's self. For some, it comes naturally, but for me, it did not, playing with my toddler and talking in a way they could understand. I was amazed at how well our daughter could talk to and entertain our son; that was a real gift in my book.

Not that I was not a child once myself, but that was so long ago, and now, it was hard to put myself in their place, hear, see, and understand in a way they could comprehend what I was trying to communicate. I had seen other people, men and women alike, who are so good at this, and I envied them. Gratefully, this frustration went away as my children grew older, and we were on a more level communication ground of understanding.

Discipline is such an important component of parenting, teaching your child right from wrong, establishing boundaries, and providing a safe and secure place for them to grow.

I remember well my parents disciplining me. Mom would instruct and correct and end it with "you just wait until your father gets home." My father was a spanker, with great emphasis, and I feared this punishment. He had left hand prints on my bottom side. I had to get smart, fast.

I know in today's world this could be considered child abuse. It was not then, and abuse was not the intended purpose. Correction and obedience were the purpose. Those days, the general social conscious about disciplining your child was different. But even more so was it different when my father was growing up. I remember hearing that when he was a child, he was not allowed to talk at all at the dinner table. Once he did, his father would hit him across the face, knocking him off his chair to the floor. Sadly, even today, not only do we learn good, but also some bad habits of our parents. Fortunate are those who turn the corner and walk a different path.

Spankings diminished as I grew older, but we did have our share of yelling matches. One thing that stuck with me though was the repetitive use of the phrase "because I said so." I was the child with the word "why" engraved on my lips. My sister obeyed without question for the most part, but I just could not stop myself from asking, "Why?" I know this frustrated my parents, and I may have over used it at times just to goad them. But truly, I really wanted to know the reasoning and purpose.

I swore I would never tell my children "because I said so." Well, truth be known, small children just look at you funny when you are in the process of giving them this glorious explanation, and in frustration I would give up and say those dreaded words, "because I said so." Funny thing is, they were good with that! Sometimes dead-end absolutes are just the best. There were times however that we intentionally, with disciplined control, employed "the wooden spoon."

As our children grew into a place of understanding, we did explain why we set rules and boundaries on them. Sometimes they had questions, and we would talk it through. We found that by engaging them in this kind of conversation, they had real actual thoughts on the subject. This led us to asking them, "What do you think the rule should be?" After listening to them, we followed up with another question, "What do you think the consequence of doing it that way might be." Finally, "Are you willing to accept that as your consequence?" We would offer our thoughts on how it should be handled and consequences that could result. In the end, we came to a conclusion that was agreeable for everyone and that everyone would respect.

We were not Dr. Spock enthusiasts (thank heaven) and certainly did not claim to be child rearing experts. We floundered as much as the next person, not knowing the right, best, perfect, and infallible way to handle each situation. Heaven forbid, we make a mistake and ruin their lives forever! We both came from a place of wanting and needing respect, harmony, and peace, and ultimately, kids want that too. Home is a great place when there is mutual love and respect. What I still find amazing was the perspective of my children. The thoughts about and solutions for situations. Parental dictatorship, for us, was not the answer. When we, as parents, were wrong, we said so to our kids and asked for their forgiveness. This opened the door for them to admit wrongdoing and know that they were still loved and worthy of forgiveness.

Parenting is an ongoing learning curve. Just when you think things are good and settled and everyone is happy, a new situation arrives at your doorstep. As much as you, at the time, desire things to run smooth, the day comes, as it now has for me, when you look back and see just how much God used ordinary, everyday situations to stretch and grow me. All these learning experiences were just preparation for the "next" place in my life. God is so good He does not waste anything but multiplies everything, for His glory, when we live life, allowing God to lead, and we, follow, in obedience to His perfect will.

Our children are adults. They are still our children, and we are still "parents." When problems arise, and they do and always will, we still engage in the two-way conversation. Tempting as it is sometimes to just tell them what to do, we choose, for the most part, not to. As we did then, we do now, we encourage them to process the information and arrive at conclusions that have integrity and are God honoring.

It is easy to succumb to the feeling that "I am not needed." I have been there at times, as it concerns my adult children. Actually, I have not been needed. I have felt sorry for myself, nursed my hurt feelings, and shed a few tears. But this is not a good place to stay for very long; it is too destructive in so many ways. Here is what I have learned, and embraced, yes, reluctantly sometime. My kids are adults. Not only do they want to, but they are fully capable of handling the situations that come up in their lives. And they do! I am so proud of them.

Here is my takeaway. I love my kids, always, forever, to the moon and back, and more. This is not just human love generated by me. It is a God-given love. It is a right, it is a privilege, it is a blessed gift from God, and it is mine, not to keep, but to generously give to them. Hannah, in the Old Testament, was childless and prayed and vowed,

> And she made this vow: "O Lord of Heaven's Armies, if you will look upon my sorrow and answer my prayer and give me a son, then I will give him back to you. He will be yours for his entire lifetime, and as a sign that he has been dedicated to the Lord, his hair will never be cut." (1 Samuel 1:11NLT)

She asked God for a son, and in gratitude, when Samuel was born, she dedicated him to service of the Lord under the care of the Priest Eli.

When I found out, each time, that I was pregnant, before they were even born, I gave my children to God, not in the same way Hannah did, but I prayed every day of their lives that God would help them to become all that He created them to be. I still pray this prayer.

I believe that God is continually answering this prayer of my heart. I believe that God used David and I to teach, instruct, guide, nurture, love, and let them go. We were not, and are not, parenting experts, but we gave back to God what He had given us, the lives of our children, that they might become all that God has created them to be.

My kids are not perfect. How could they be? Their parents certainly are not. They make wrong choices, go down the wrong paths, and receive the consequences. But I know, they do not stay there. By God's grace, mercy, and love, He leads them through their valleys, to the green pastures and the still waters.

I believe that my children, like us their parents, have not arrived. We are all a work in process, stretched and grown every day that we draw breath on this earth until He calls us home! Praise God!

Once a parent, always a parent, and now even, grandparents.

CHAPTER 14

The Empty Nest

Perspective: the empty nest. Having children just naturally brings life milestones. For some that includes day care, four-year-old kindergarten, but for us it started with kindergarten. Elementary school for our kids went through the sixth grade. Middle school was next for three years, high school for three years, and then moving away from home for college for four years.

How these years play out is ordered by not only their academic requirements but also the activities they choose to be involved in. The life skills they acquire along the way will continue to stretch and grow throughout their adult lives. Navigating relationships in multiple personal, spiritual, academic, and social settings are foundational to their confidence, courage, and sense of self-worth as they take on the challenges of the world they live in.

Essential to their growth is a strong home and family foundation. It is not up to the school to raise your child. God gives clear direction to parents in Proverbs:

...train up a child in the way he should go, and when he is old, he will not depart from it. (Proverbs 22:6 NKJV)

This is not a promise that your child will never mess up, but again, instruction to parents. Parents are to be active in showing by example in the way you conduct and live your life and being consistent in daily instruction that guides them to finding the purpose for which God has created them.

Schools and teachers provide an education for your child. In addition to academics, they provide guidance, boundaries, support, and direction for your child to transition into the world as a responsible, productive, contributing adult.

Parenting and education must work cooperatively together. Teachers supporting parents and parents supporting teachers. They each see the child in different settings and situations, and children can respond differently in both. But give them credit. Kids know dissention and division when they see it, and they know how to use it.

Our children filled our calendar with activity, and David was the keeper of the family calendar. It was important to our involvement in their lives, from making sure they had lunch money to attending school events, helping with homework, assisting with the paper route, taking them to youth group and church, or accomplishing household chores. It also allowed us to frame out time to do things together. During their younger years, we enjoyed going to family camp in Rhinelander, Wisconsin, during the summer, and though not many, we did take a few family vacations together. With my sister living in North Carolina, we made multiple trips there and did special things together while in the area. Visiting the Biltmore in Ashville was one of our favorites, and we managed to see it in three different seasons.

Before we knew it, the kids were driving, had jobs, and social lives with friends. With both of us working full-time jobs, we could not be everywhere all the time. A car was purchased for them to share. In fact, when the first car rusted and the engine block dropped, we purchased a second car that not only took both of them through college but was passed on to our nephew where it finally met its end in a tornado that went through his college campus.

High school graduation is a momentous event, not only for the graduate, but for mom and dad. We were so proud. The families gathered, friends came, and a party was held to celebrate the accomplishments, twice. There is a distinct difference in the emotions between your first child graduating high school and your second. With the second comes the permeance that a season of life had ended. New emotions were on the horizon, and sometimes it felt like a whirlwind.

You remember back to the days of diapers and midnight feedings when you thought it would never end, and then, standing before you in cap and gown is your child, grown up, and on the precipice of going out into the world alone. Where did that time go? What seemed so slow once whizzed past so fast it left you breathless. My mother used to tell me to not rush things; they are young only once and all too soon they are gone.

Moving our daughter four hours away to college was one of the biggest life changes since she entered our lives eighteen years earlier. She was a young eighteen-year old, not even a month past her eighteenth birthday, and we were dropping her off at the Taylor University, Fort Wayne, Indiana college campus, moving her precious belongings into a dorm room, in a big city. It was emotional to say the least. We hugged and said our good-byes. She teared up, turned, and walked away. Together with our son, we climbed into the rented van and headed home. We stopped at the welcome center just as we reentered Wisconsin, sat on a bench, and cried, all three of us.

Many were the phone calls that ensued. They were wonderful, hard, and sometimes downright exhausting. Parent's weekend came and it was the first of many trips to college, including taking my parents for grandparents' weekend. It was exciting for them to see the young adult their first grandchild had become. Though it was exciting to see our daughter, saying good-bye left a hole in our hearts. It was right, but it was hard.

Both of our children chose Taylor University. The first year for our daughter was at the smaller Fort Wayne campus, bigger city, but her second year, she transferred to the larger main campus in the smaller town of Upland, Indiana.

A few weeks after returning home after her third year in college, our son graduated high school. This high school graduation brought a new emotion to the mix. School days, as we had known them for the past sixteen years, were done, gone. Accomplishment, success, celebration, yes, absolutely. We teetered on the edge of our next big life change.

By the end of the summer, we were moving both of our children to college, and this time, they drove together in their car, and we had the van full of their stuff. It is just hard work moving kids into a dorm, with no air conditioning, in August, at the height of summer heat and humidity. It seemed our daughter was always on the third or fourth floor, but our son lucked out getting a ground-level, air-conditioned dorm. This was a blessing for him as he inherited my plethora of allergies. And so began a significant year for each of us.

Amiee was starting her last year of college, Austin his first, and we traveled back home to an empty house.

Their year together in college was exciting on so many levels. It strengthened their relationship, becoming independent, but dependent all in the same breath. We made multiple trips to Upland that year for special parent weekends. The memories from that year were as much fun as they were precious. The end of May arrived quickly, and we were attending our daughter's college graduation. Tears of pride and joy filled my eyes.

Amiee secured a job that summer and continued to live at home. She bought her first car, and Austin now had their car all to himself. By August we were moving Austin back to college, a family affair. This time Austin had the car on campus and was making his way alone. This too was an emotionally hard letting go as a mom. It was the first time Austin was away from home on his own. He was friendly and social and became involved in theater. Austin was always a hard worker and nonetheless during his college career. He was also our adventurer and made the most of his adventures with his friends. I instructed him to only share these adventures after he was back and safe.

It was nice having Amiee back home, but it was very different. She was a responsible adult. Had a life of her own, and though we shared the same space, our home, new boundaries went in place, both for her and for us.

David and I started to "date" again when our nest became empty. We tried things we had not previously experienced, and one we enjoyed was attending performances at the UW Whitewater Campus, at their Irving Young Performing Arts Center. We could go out for dinner, shopping, or like we always enjoyed, just taking rides. It was a time of growing in our relationship, in a different season of life.

CHAPTER 15

A Leap of Faith

Perspective: adventure, a leap of faith. The summer before Austin started his third year of college, we came upon yet another life-changing opportunity. Friends of ours lived in Colorado Springs and ran a CBRF. They had informed us of a Christian bookstore up the mountain in Woodland Park that was going to be sold. I have known these friends since I was a teenager, and they had played a significant role in our lives prior to their moving to Colorado. Colorado was special to them as they had met there many years prior when they were both working at a family camp in the mountains.

They encouraged us to come out and at least take a look at this possible business opportunity. We took a couple days off work, leaving after work and driving straight through, arriving in Colorado the following morning. Coming into Colorado Springs, we saw the sun rising on the mountains, and it was a sight unlike any other. We stayed in the home of our friends' mother, and they showed us around Colorado Springs up the mountain to Woodland Park and introduced us to the owner of the bookstore. It was a picture-perfect, absolutely beautiful store.

Needless to say, we were excited on our trip home. We took the matter to God and prayed for His guidance, asking Him to open the doors and provide a way if this was His will for our lives. At the time I was working for an attorney in town, and David was employed locally also. We were not flushed with financial capital, had never been business owners, and basically had no idea what to do first. David spent a lot of time in conversation with our friends in Colorado; they were, after all, experienced in owning businesses, and this was not their first.

As we obtained their advice, followed their suggestions, worked with the current owners, and prayed, a lot, God started opening the doors and shining His light on the path. This was nothing less than a huge leap of faith for us, and the day came when we said "yes" to this new call on our lives.

My parents were not at all happy. For years we had lived just three blocks away from them and they had become dependent on us but were still able to function independently. It was hard for them to have my sister living in North Carolina, but now, we were making a move to Colorado. A sense of loss was felt by them.

David's parents were more accepting, largely because as a minister, dad had stayed with a church about seven years before pulling up stakes and moving on to another location. They had been through this, and it was more the norm.

We tried selling our house, but that was not God's plan. Instead, He found renters for us. Preparation for this move, now to be our eighth, was much greater than previous moves. We had close to twenty years of accumulated stuff, not to mention everything our kids had.

This was going to be a big change for Amiee too as she had to find a place to live. She could not afford to rent our home while we were gone, and unfortunately, we needed the income. I hoped Amiee would find a nice apartment, safe and secure, but the rent for such was beyond her budget. She found a place out on Lake

Koshkonong, a small duplex, and she rented the upper portion. It was not at all what I imagined which made it hard for me to leave her there. We got her packed up, moved, and settled in. Amiee made the best of it and in the process stretched and grew in her own independence.

We started the process of sorting through stuff, holding a rummage sale, and deciding what would go and what would stay to be stored in my parent's attic. Austin had to come home from college as we wanted him involved in making decisions about his stuff. Basically, he packed it all and it went to my parent's attic. It was just too much to decide in a short span of time.

I resigned from my position at the law office, and though we had negotiated with David's employer to have him work for them in Colorado, last minute they decided to terminate his employment. This threw us for a loop, but then, God knew this was coming, and we now simply had only one choice. Trust God!

I had been busy packing us up, and finally the day of our eighth move arrived. Our friends from Colorado flew home to ride with us and help us with the move. Truck and car loaded, we headed out for Colorado. It was the end of October when we left and we arrived in Colorado the first of November.

We had not secured a place to live, so we moved all our belongings into a storage unit. With our clothes, we moved into our friend's mother's basement. It was nicely finished with our own living room, dining area, bedroom, bath, and laundry. We did however share the kitchen for some cooking.

Our first month in Colorado was consumed with buying the bookstore and setting up our business. We were so blessed to have our friend's years of experience, walking us through each step, connecting us with a lawyer, and making sure that everything was set up correctly.

We both started working in the store, getting acquainted with the business, vendors, sales, marketing, and employees. We were fortunate to be able to rent the space from the previous owner who had one year left on his contract with the property owner. The store was located in a small mall complex in Woodland Park, about a half hour up the mountain from Colorado Springs.

The store was open six days a week, and on Sunday mornings we attended church and took drives in the afternoon, exploring. We had to do some serious apartment shopping so we could get moved into a place of our own. This was successful, and just before Thanksgiving, we once again loaded up the truck for our nineth move, out of storage into an apartment.

It was a beautiful apartment, newer, on the third floor, with an outside entrance and no elevator. We had two bedrooms, two bathrooms, nice kitchen, dining, and living room with a spacious patio. Per my norm, I had us unpacked and settled in under three days. A small storage unit came with the apartment which was perfect for our refrigerator, stove, washer, and dryer as these were provided in the apartment.

I remember the move well. It took the good part of the day to just get the truck loaded and make several trips to the new apartment. By the last trip it was dark, it had snowed, the roads were slippery, and we had a big hill to climb to get to the apartment. My sense of direction has never been good, and, honestly, if I do not follow the same path, I get lost. I had not driven this route to our apartment, but the last trip, I had to. As long as I could follow David, life was good. But just before the climb up that hill was a stop light. With a running start, it would be ok, and David made it through, but I did not. Not only did I struggle up that slippery hill, but I had lost tract of David. He became aware that I was not behind him, and watchful soul that he is, he pulled over and waited for me. I was so grateful; words could not express.

We spent Thanksgiving alone that year. I fixed a dinner with all the fixings, and we began to feel settled. Next came preparations for Christmas. We kept most of the employees on and they were a huge help. Between them, they had pretty much run the store. The previous owner liked to buy and decorate, but not handle the day-to-day things. I had been the assistant manager of a Gold Crown Hallmark Store and received training through them in advertising, display, pricing, purchasing, sales, and marketing. Other experience working in radio broadcast, sales, marketing, advertising, and department management from previous positions had well prepared me for business ownership. I felt confident in holding up my end of our adventure.

David handled all the bookkeeping, invoices, communication with vendors, creditors, and payroll taxes, as well as ensuring our POS systems were all working correctly. Together we worked in the store, and David enjoyed the interaction with customers.

It was so much fun dressing the store for Christmas. Sales were good, but it became clear really quick that the store was barely able to support itself and pay salaries. Unfortunately, we had to cut hours for some employees, and I worked without a paycheck.

We had arranged with our kids to come to our new home for Christmas. Together they made the long trek to Colorado Springs. We had a live Christmas tree that year that had been grown in our home state of Wisconsin. It was a special Christmas. We enjoyed showing them around Colorado Springs, Woodland Park, and doing some hiking. Unlike Wisconsin, it was sunny and warm and conducive to sitting on the patio and doing things outside.

This was the year that went from 1999 to 2000, Y2K, and there was concern about the transition of computers, and all things national security, New Year's Eve, Y2K. With NORAD nearby, and the Air Force base, additional foreign personnel were present in Colorado Springs, and security was heightened.

Every New Year's Eve, fireworks are shot off from Pikes Peak. We stayed up and were able to go out on the breezeway and watch the fireworks. It was quite a spectacular sight. The evening passed to New Year's Day, 2000 without incident.

Amiee had to get back to work and Austin back to college. We packed them up and sent them on their way. Our full house became empty once again. Just as we were getting ready to settle into our new routine, David received a call from his old boss. They wanted to hire him back and have him work from Colorado.

This was such a God thing. We needed those two months with David giving his full attention to our bookstore, getting it set up, making sure everything was functioning as it should. We also had some financial concerns if David was not going to be able to draw a salary, but God had that handled. God is so good. He met all of our needs.

The next few months were full and challenging. With David now working for the company in Wisconsin, he had to fly back to Wisconsin several times, leaving me alone in Colorado. He was always back within the week, and remarkably I managed. Learning to drive up and down that mountain was challenging. It was steep and narrow and experienced drivers drove much faster than me. Spring meant snow, a lot of snow. The passages on the road up to Woodland Park were not plowed well, so it was slippery and treacherous. One particular day, and David was not in Wisconsin, I asked him to drive me up the mountain, but he assured me I would be ok. I set off on my own. It took me an hour and a half to just get up the mountain, a trip that was normally about a half hour. I got to the store parking lot, drove in, drove out, and spent another hour and a half driving back down the mountain. This was the single, most frightening drive I have ever made in my life. I have driven in Wisconsin winters and snow that were not fun, but this was the worst.

I had altitude issues while living in Colorado. Coming down the mountain my ears would plug up and stay plugged for several hours, every day. I struggle with breathing, and climbing the six flights of stairs to get to our third-floor apartment left me breathless. In addition, I experienced nausea, headaches, and dizziness.

The atmosphere is very dry. It did not matter how much I drank and tried to hydrate; my skin not only dried out but cracked open. I learned from an herbalist that I needed to hydrate from the inside with more than water. Following their recommendation of Evening Prime Rose Oil seemed to help. The water contained such harsh mineral content that it left orange stains in the shower, and my hair was dryer than normal.

I plunged myself into the work of the store. Many families that live in the mountains home school. We had received requests for curriculum, so after researching it, David and I decided to start a home school curriculum section in our store. We had books, music, a children's corner, and cards and gifts, but this home school curriculum outsold them all. It literally made our store profitable. It was a blessing to us and to many families who, prior to our stocking the curriculum, had to drive as far as Denver to get what they needed. This too was a God thing.

A tragedy touched our staff. Two daughters, ages 12 and 14, of one of our employees were crossing the highway to catch their bus to school. It was not quite dawn, and both were struck by a car, which happened to be driven by the school liaison officer. Visibility was not good. It was a tragic accident. One died at the scene, and the other later in the hospital. Why God?

How on earth do you move forward?

Their funeral was unlike any we have attended. Both girls knew and loved Jesus, Praise God for that. There was a celebration of their lives, and glory was given to God. What a testimony to the over 1,000 parents, students, friends, and family attending. The impact on my life will forever be with me. For the family, only God knows.

By March David and I decided it would be better if we could live in Woodland Park where our store was located. With him now having to travel it just made sense for me to be closer, eliminating the mountain drive. The search began for a place to live, and we found a wonderful duplex on the edge of town owned by a lovely older couple who lived next door. By our anniversary in May, our 25th no less, we had made our tenth move. We had to climb stairs to get into the duplex, but we had some wonderful strong young movers with Two Men and a Truck to do the heavy work. Prior to the big move, I had packed boxes, loaded the car, and every day moved a little bit more by myself into our new home. By the time the furniture arrived, I had us settled. We went out for a special celebratory anniversary dinner.

This move made sense in so many ways. Closer to our store, our church was in Woodland Park, the rent was less, and I no longer had to deal with the ups and downs of the mountain with driving or my ears. The bonus was the setting: pine trees, beautiful flowers, humming birds, no bugs, and sitting on our patio you could see Pikes Peak.

I remember well David's first trip to Wisconsin after we had moved to Woodland Park. I had enjoyed walking around our neighborhood; it was not far but just enough to get me outside. On one such walk, I encounter, not real close, but close enough, a herd of Elk. They are huge. I had no issue, but I scaled the walk down. When David was gone, I tended to stay up later because I could not sleep. Shortly after the Elk encounter, late night TV went to a blue screen. Up came a warning to people to keep their children and small animals inside and well attended if they were outside. Black bears were coming out of hibernation, and they were hungry. It was also a more active time for mountain lions. I never walked again.

There had been evidence of bear activity at night between our house and the landlords. He had seen it before. He had a birdbath, and the bear liked to have a drink, tipping it over in the process. We were also cautioned to keep our grill in the garage, as well as any garbage containers. These attracted bear as well. One-night after we had gone to bed, we were woken up by a noise on the house. Our bedroom was on the second floor, in the loft. This happened a couple of times. Finally, one night we found out what was making the noise. A family of racoons came up the steps, onto the deck, climbed up the siding, onto the roof. David hauled out our super soaker and shot water at them to chase them away. It seemed to work for a while.

Come the end of May, college was out and it was time for us to move Austin home for the summer. We drove all the way to Upland, Indiana, and between his car and ours packed everything he owned into both. It was very creative. As we were approaching Colorado Springs, the sun had almost set and we could see the lights of the city against the mountain. A noise was heard, and we quickly deduced that we had a flat tire and pulled over. By the side of the road, with only light from a flash light, we unloaded a very full trunk, got the tools and the spare tire out, changed the tire (one of those small just get you through tires), repacked the trunk, and headed, very slowly, up the mountain to home. Exhausted, we locked up the cars and crashed for the night, settling him in the next day.

It was a special summer. Austin worked with us at the bookstore and in doing so completed a work study project for college. He helped us work through and complete an extensive inventory. The last time I had worked with my son was on his paper route in elementary school. What a change!

With Austin we embarked on our first trip up Pikes Peak. We had seen cars and trucks drive the road from our patio and decided it was time we go. David was driving, Austin was in the back seat, and we set off. Driving in the mountains was always a tense thing, and this was no different, until we got beyond the tree line. David came around a bend in the road, the mountain was to our left, but in front and to the right, there was nothing by sky, and no guard rails. He stopped, broke out in a sweat, and said, "I can't do this." There was panic in his voice.

Not long before this we had read of someone who panicked on this road, but when trying to step on the break, had hit the gas, and gone over the edge. How quickly this came to mind as I was looking at David.

I said, "Austin, dad needs help, he does not look good." Austin came behind his dad, put his hands on his shoulders while calmly and quietly talking in his ear, guided David to turn the car around, and headed back down to the tree line where there was a rest stop, wayside, break check point. We parked the car and went inside, had something to drink, used the restrooms, watched some movies about Pikes Peak. An hour later we headed back down the mountain.

We made it up Pikes Peak, but we took the Cog Railway up. It was a beautiful ride. A guide talked along the way, and we saw long-horned sheep and finally arrive at the top, 12,000 or so feet. There was a restaurant and information site and places to walk around. David and Austin were just fine, even walking over to an edge they pointed out where we lived. That did it for me. I got dizzy, needed the restroom, and I couldn't breathe. David got me some French fries, and I got back on the Cog and waited for the return down the mountain. Amazing effect the thin air and altitude have on your body.

We went on hikes together and explored different towns, parks, and tourist sites of Colorado. It was the summer Austin turned twenty-one, and it was memorable. I especially enjoyed having Austin around when David was in Wisconsin. Austin is an awesome cook, and I reaped the benefits. Thunderstorms up on the mountain were unlike any I have seen. Bolts of lightning were big, bright, loud, and frightening. It seemed that when David was gone, we had storms and I was grateful that I was not alone.

During these summer months forest fires broke out on the mountain. It was very dry, and even in our backyard, dead pine needles covered the ground. We learned that is just the way it was.

There were two fires that could possibly cause a threat to us. I had lived in Wisconsin and experienced tornado action, but a forest fire was a whole other beast, and it scared me. Not only could we smell the fires, we could see the clouds of smoke. One was twenty-five miles away, and a smaller one was down the main highway about five miles.

Before summers end, the fires had been put out. We were able to take a drive to the area of the fire that had been twenty-five miles away. We have never seen such devastation. Fire is no respecter of people, homes or property. It was an eye opener for the three of us.

The summer passed quickly and before we knew it, we were packing Austin up to return to college. He downsized a bit and we were able to get everything into his car, and he drove back to college alone. It was hard to let him go.

Through our church we met a wonderful couple, Roy and Margaret, who worked full time in a ministry for Pastors and their wives and other ministry leaders, called SonScape. They had a retreat center where couples would come to refocus, renew, refresh, and deepen their walk with God, both in their relationship and in their ministry.

We were treated to a weekend at SonScape. It was an awesome experience in which David and I reconnected in a deeper, meaningful way. Colorado was a daily walk of faith, and this weekend brought clarity, purpose, and vision to our marriage and our relationship together with God.

The property lease on our bookstore was coming to an end for the previous owner and it would now become our responsibility to take it over. Terms of the lease changed, the rent was greater, and the length of commitment longer. We had to face a challenging reality: we simply could not afford to sign this lease.

We looked for alternative locations, even back down in Colorado Springs, but it just was not meant to be. First time ever I was experiencing being "home sick." We questioned why God would bring us all this way just to end it after only a year. We prayed, along with our staff and friends. When it became clear that we could not relocate, we tried to sell the business. Our time frame was limited. What little interest we had fell through, and we had no choice but to go out of business and sell what assets we could.

It was a huge blessing when a church in Colorado Springs heard of our sale and were interested in purchasing all of our fixtures to start a library. Our fixtures were all crafted out of cherry wood and were beautiful. There were a couple of antiques that I would have loved to keep, but it just wasn't reasonable for us to do so, and we sold them also.

We had a "going out of business" sale. Having worked in retail before, experiencing after Christmas and sidewalk sales, I knew this would be challenging. For some reason people think you should practically give stuff away, arguing with you to lower the price and demonstrating no concern for your need to make some profit. I did not enjoy this side of people and I needed God's grace, and He was generous.

We were able to sell a large portion of our inventory, but what we couldn't, we packed up in boxes and moved it with us. We had received direction from God to move back to Wisconsin, and God confirmed this to us time and again by answered prayers. Every day of our walk through this process began and ended with faith. We saw impossibilities, but God provided possibilities.

But, the lease on our home back in Wisconsin was not up! Where would we live? Well, God had an answer to that also. The renters reneged on the lease and moved out three months before it was up. With David traveling to Wisconsin, he was able to work through details, preparing for our return.

The renters, though they did not destroy the home, had left damage behind. All the downstairs carpet had to be ripped out. David found hardwood floors under the carpet that were in doable condition. They had multiple pets in the house so thorough cleaning had to be done. Upstairs carpets were shampooed, and walls, wood-work, and cupboards washed. When David was in Wisconsin, he spent evenings and weekends, along with help from Amiee, getting the house ready for us to move back in.

I was busy packing us up for move eleven. Everything but the essentials was in boxes. Our move date was the last day of November. Our friends, Roy and Margaret, invited us to their home for Thanksgiving. They are awesome in the kitchen and it was one of the best Thanksgiving dinners we have ever had. Other friends and family were there also, and the fellowship was to praise God for!

A friend from Wisconsin came to drive one of our cars back home with us. We had help from church men and friends to load our U-Haul and help us get the boxes from the store secured as well. The morning of our departure from the mountain, there was hail descending from heaven, and the noise on the car, while driv-ing down the mountain, was frightening. David drove the truck, I was in a car behind him, and our friend was driving the other car behind me. Being in the middle, I wouldn't get lost. It was a long day, and as night fell, we were in Omaha, Nebraska. I am no good at navigating, anywhere, period. I rode the bumper of the truck so that David could not see me in the side mirrors. Cars and lights were everywhere, and I had reached my limit of stress. Once through the city David stopped for the night. I was grateful.

December first, the last leg of the drive home, we crossed into Wisconsin, the sun was shining, it was warm out, and my heart was rejoicing. God brought us home, my heart was full, my life was changed. We had dinner and spent the night at my mom's and the next day began the task of unloading and settling in. Yes, I had us settled by the end of the second day. That house, that became our home, was holding us in its arms again, and it was wonderful.

That weekend, we moved Amiee back home. Where she had been living, the tenant downstairs smoked, and her things had absorbed the odor. We washed absolutely everything. She was glad to be back in her room, and we had missed her so much, it was good to be together again.

Wisconsin welcomed us with a big old snowstorm. Somehow, Wisconsin snow is just friendlier. I did not mind doing the snow blowing. David was back to work, and I started preparing for Christmas and job hunting.

Austin came home for his Christmas break and partially moved back into his room, though most everything was either in his college dorm or my mom's attic. What he had left behind in Colorado with us we had already set up in his room, which included a bed to sleep in. It was nice having our whole family together again, in our home. While home, Austin helped me sort through all the inventory we brought home and make a master list of it all. David would work off this list to call vendors and see what we might be able to return. Once that portion was complete, David made arrangements for paying off the debt we still owed them. A time came that some of the vendors forgave the debt. Another blessing from God.

After going through what was left, and keeping some that we wanted, we contacted a church near Milwaukee that had a store house for missionaries. When home, missionaries could go through and take what would be useful on the mission field when they returned. We were overjoyed when they showed up with a couple of vans and took what was left of our inventory. It was a joy to donate to such a worthy cause and a double joy for them to receive it. God always has a plan.

I had a couple of job interviews that did not pan out, and then one came up that I really thought I would like. It was the office administration position at the elementary school, across the street from my parents that we all had gone to. I was excited to be granted an interview. I was sure this was where God would take me. So close to home I could walk. It was quite a letdown when I received the call that I was not hired. God must have something else, something better. Faith.

Within a weeks' time, I received a call from the principal at the school. The person she hired worked one day and quit. Now she would have to post the job again for two weeks but asked if I would be willing to come in and work those two weeks and go through another interview. Of course, I said yes, I knew God's hand was in this. I started the following Monday. When the two weeks were up, I went through another interview and was offered the job.

It had been an interesting two weeks. The work to be done was manageable, and I picked up on things quickly. But I had witnessed a dynamic in the office that caused me to pause. I told the principal I would like to just talk it over with David and I would let her know the next day. We came to the conclusion that for whatever reason, this could not be how things always were. Just bad timing. David asked if I liked the principal, and did I feel I could do the work. Yes, to both of them. We prayed, and the next day I called back and accepted the position.

CHAPTER 16

No Turning Back

Perspective: no turning back, a funeral and weddings. Settling into a new season and routine was soon to change again. Austin graduated college in May. After seven years of college being a major role in our lives, it, too, was now gone. We moved him home where he stayed for a little over a month. It was like old times, but it really wasn't. Both kids, or better put adult children, had jobs, schedules, routines, and commitments. Austin's new job was a distant drive for him. He was proactive in finding a place closer to work, and he moved out on his own. This was a good thing, but we missed him more than a little.

Before we knew it, we had been back home a year and it was Christmas again. Now Amiee had not dated a lot, so when she said she had met Kevin on line, and he would be coming New Year's Eve, we found ourselves surprised. It seemed out of character for our daughter, but not out of character for God to move in mysterious ways. This ushered in yet another season of life.

They became engaged, and navigated, not only a long-distance relationship, but also planning a wedding and building a home, out of state. The months were filled with excitement, exhaustion, appointments, decisions, tension, deadlines, and the creation of a new family, in our family. So typical of all life experiences, a first time for everything, and no user-friendly manual to follow. It is one thing to plan your own wedding but quite another to participate in the planning of your daughter's. Another learning curve for us.

Getting to this place in our lives meant overcoming some health challenges with David. After the first TIA stroke and resolution of high blood pressure, David had two more significant TIAs. Each time the treatment for blood pressure increased. Stress management was also incorporated. While living at the higher altitudes in Colorado, frequent flights to Wisconsin, David's blood pressure remain at dangerous high levels, and sleeping lying down became more difficult.

During the year and a half after returning to Wisconsin, the sleeping improved, but not the blood pressure and he had another borderline TIA. It was suggested and recommended by our health insurance company and our family doctor that David should go to Mayo Clinic. Arrangements were made and we headed to Rochester, Minnesota. Within a couple of days, after many tests, medication changes, and a lot of prayer, David's blood pressure was lowered to not just acceptable but normal range. We had much to be grateful for.

Though our news was good, while at Mayo Clinic we received word that David's mom, who had been battling cancer, had a fall due to weakness, was in the hospital, and had passed and gone to meet her Savior. Though a blessing that Amiee and Kevin were able to visit her earlier that summer, she would not be with us to celebrate their marriage.

After the funeral, along with David's brothers, we helped his dad with things around the house, getting things set so he would be able to continue living in their home. Dad was very handy in many ways and never one to shy away from a challenge. Life without mom would be his greatest challenge.

The year passed quickly, and it seemed May was always to be an eventful month for our family. Amiee was (and I might be just a bit prejudice) a breathtakingly beautiful bride. We had so many moments of pride and joy over the years with our kids, and here yet was still another new one for us. Our little girl, a grown woman, was married and moving five hours away from us, and we had a son-in-law. Letting her go was not easy, after all we had always been her go to for everything, but now, she had Kevin, and we felt a hole in our lives. How time and precious moments just seem to fly by.

Not to let the dust settle, before this summer would come to a close, Austin, who also had not dated a lot, met that someone special, but she was a local girl, and he did not meet her on line. As she was starting college, we thought there would be a bit of time, but come fall, they were engaged, with wedding plans for, you guessed it, the next May.

Another year passed quickly as wedding plans were again in motion, though this time we were less involved we were still able to support. I found myself wondering how it was possible that my son, who in his own special way had filled my life with many precious memories, was getting married. Where did the years go? Each significant event in your youngest child's life brings with it a sense of finality, this wedding day was no different, and for me, this time, letting go was harder. I am not sure why and I do not know how to explain it. Our son was married and we had a daughter-in-law.

In a short time, though our family was bigger, the "empty nest" was a true, no turning back, reality. We had invested time, energy, resources, instruction, disciplines, guidance, education, and all of our love into our kids. They had achieved and mastered goals in life that are the hope and dream of every parent. They were accomplished, responsible adults. Yes, so much to celebrate, pride burst our seams, but in the same breath, our arms felt empty and our hearts were lonely. Reflecting on the events of their lives, I was reminded again of what my mother used to say when they were small and I just could not wait for *fill in the blank*. Mom would tell me, "Enjoy these moments, do not rush them, they grow up so fast, and one day, you are going to miss this." Very wise words that I now find myself telling my children.

Now, with both children married and in homes of their own, we took a hard look at the place we now were at in our lives. David's job had him driving an hour and a half, one way, to work every day. I was fortunate to be three blocks away from my job and could walk. Between the traffic and time away from home, the journey wore him down. With both the kids living, Austin, out of town and Amiee, out of state, we started looking for a place to live, midway between both our jobs, and in no time at all we found a newly built home. In the same amount of no time at all, we sold our house. The market was good. There I was, packing us up for our twelfth move, which we made in the summer, just in time to be done before school started in September. We loved the house, the location, the neighborhood, but, my three blocks turned into a forty-five-minute drive, the reality of which did not really sink in until winter arrived in all its snowy glory. David's hour and a half one way whittled down to forty-five-minutes, and it coordinated so that we left and returned about the same time each day. In the long run, it was good.

CHAPTER 17

When Parents Die

Perspective: when parents die. Changes that come with growing older have a permanent way of altering life. You never really figure it all out. Just when you think you got it, something new shows up on your doorstep. There are some changes unfortunately you must learn to accept and live with even when you are young, hopeful, and indestructible.

David and I had both experienced the death of a grandparent, great aunts, and uncles, those members of the family that just got old. But we also had walked through the valleys of those taken too soon. Some of these were classmates in high school, some with people we worked with or knew through our church, and some, family. Those taken too soon, for various reasons, seem to stick out in your memory and are the most difficult to reconcile in your mind. We had even helped both of our parents as their mothers and fathers (our grandparents) had passed. Assisting with the taking apart of a household, sorting, moving, and dispersing. The full weight of the burden was not on our shoulders, until the day came when it was.

I must step back for a moment here. You will remember how as a child I spent weekends and weeks during the summer on my grandma and grandpa's farm. For me, grandma and grandpa held a very special spot in my heart. My first experience of letting go of someone I loved happened when my grandpa died when I was fifteen. I did not know much about death and I was curious. Grandpa looked the same in that casket. I reached out to hold his hand. It was stone cold. Yes, I should have known, but I did not. It was shock and surprise. It was cold. It hurt. It was death.

When my children were in high school, I had another significant encounter with death. My grandma was in the nursing home where I worked as a department head. I was able to visit her every day. We talked a lot and I witnessed significant changes in my sweet grandma. I attribute the loss of her filter to the stroke. In this time though I also saw strengths in her that I identified not only in my own mother, but myself. We were women of independence and tenacious strength.

It was a Sunday morning. Mom called me to let me know the nursing home had called and felt that we should come and be with grandma. Mom asked if I would go with her and I did. Grandma was sleeping but seemed restless but did not open her eyes or wake up. Together mom and I read Psalm 23 and prayed. We told grandma it was ok if she needed to leave.

Aunt Ethel, mom's sister, came. They sat off to the side and were visiting as only my mom and Aunt Ethel could. I was sitting next to grandma. What happened next was so vivid and real and I remember it like it was yesterday. For me, it was a gift from God.

Grandma's breathing changed. Slower, peaceful. From my right, coming from the ceiling, I witnessed a bright light making its way into the room (there was no window there, it was a wall). Slowly the light moved down toward my grandma's face. I told mom and Aunt Ethel that Jesus was coming for grandma. They did not seem to respond. I told them again, but they continued to talk.

As I sat there, I witnessed the light go down and shine on grandma's face. She was full of color and life like I always remembered her. Then her breathing continued to get slower, shallow, and then gently stopped. As her breathing stopped, the light slowly started receding back up from where it came. As it did the color drained from grandma's face, almost turning gray. I could only watch, not speak or move. Within a moments time, the light was gone and the room was still.

I told mom and Aunt Ethel that grandma had just left with Jesus; she was gone. This time they did come over to the bed. A nurse was called in and confirmed that yes indeed, grandma had passed on to her heavenly home.

As cold and shocking was my grandpa's death, leaving me feel empty and sad; grandma's death was warm, loving, and filled me not only with peace but hope. God gave me a promise that day. Back now. It started with David's mom passing just ten months before Amiee's wedding. Austin had not even been married a year when we learned of my mother's pancreatic cancer. She felt off in April, went to the doctor in May, was diagnosed by two different doctors, had surgery in June, and went home to Jesus on our daughter's birthday in August.

It really all began with a phone call from my mom on Mother's Day. She was not feeling right and had yellowish look to her face. She went to the urgent care at the hospital where she was calling us from as she needed a ride home as dad was not driving anymore. It was recommended that she see her own doctor the next day. What we thought might be Hepatitis B the doctor ruled out, suspecting cancer he made an appointment for her at the hospital in Madison.

David was scheduled to go and pick mom up that afternoon after her appointment. I was at work when I received a phone call from my mom. She was in tears as she told me they said I have pancreatic cancer. The news rocked my world. My mom had been healthy most of her life.

Knowing that David was close to arriving, I quickly called him to let him know what he would be facing once he arrived. I finished things up at work and left early that day.

An appointment had been made for mom to see a specialist in Madison, so I took off work and took her and my dad to this appointment. He confirmed the diagnosis and made his recommendations for surgery. My frustration with my dad began that day at this appointment. His concern for my mother was limited to telling the doctor that he did not care what he had to do, just get her better, I need someone to cook, do laundry, and drive. I tried to pass it off as just frustration, but it rattled around in the back of my mind.

Wanting a second opinion, my mom asked around for suggestions as to where she should go and Froedtert Hospital in Milwaukee was recommended. Another appointment was made and I once again took my parents to the appointment. This in itself was challenging as it meant driving in Milwaukee which I was not skilled at. Fortunately, I have a cousin who lived near Milwaukee and she knew her way around. We met at her home and she drove us the remainder of the way to the hospital.

Surgery was again recommended, only this time a much clearer explanation was given, and mom felt better about going this route. My dad gave his same speech to this doctor which caused me to have concerns.

Surgery was scheduled for June, and mom had several appointments in preparation for the surgery that I accompanied her on. The day of the surgery, David took off work and we took both mom and dad to the hospital. We were told it could be a seven to eight-hour surgery so we went prepared to occupy our time. After only five hours, the doctor came to the waiting room to inform us that mom was out of surgery and was in recovery, and he was not able to do the full procedure as the cancer had spread to her liver. He did what he could to make her feel more comfortable. This news was devasting to me.

I remember well when we were allowed back to her room to see her. My mom's hair was very thin for many years, and she choose to wear wigs, but she was emphatic that no one should ever see her without the wig, so naturally I had not. I went into the room that was my mom's, but I did not see my mother in there. I went to the nurse station and told them that my mother was not in that room and that there was an old man in there. Assuring me that this was my mother, they walked with me to her room. Mom did not have her wig on, and I totally did not recognize her. She already looked rough from the surgery, she was sleeping, and I was shocked at what I saw.

Mom was in the hospital for a bit. My sister and husband came home for a visit. From the hospital mom was transferred to a rehab wing at the local hospital back in Fort Atkinson. Every day after work I went to visit her and gave my dad a ride back home. She met with oncology to discuss treatment options and recommended a trial treatment for her, giving her a book to read about the trial. David took the book, read it through, and then sat down and explained it all to my mom. Bottom line, her life expectancy could be extended a possible six months, no guarantee. Side effects would play a major role in the treatment. After discussion and prayer, my mom opted to not have treatment.

It was at one of these visits after work, dad was not there that day, just me and mom, and she asked me, "Carol, do you think I am going to die from this?"

Despite our many differences, mom and I shared a lot of similar characteristics, and one of those was what you see is what you get matter of fact approach to life. This was one of those moments, and it slammed me like a train hitting me. For moments I was stunned and speechless. Not wanting to be the first to utter the words, I asked the question right back to her, "What do you think?" The answer for both of us was yes.

As always, insurance drives the length of one's stay and mom had run out of days and she refused to go to a nursing home, a concept I well understand. We met with social workers who helped us make arrangements for mom to go home with in home health care. As their bedrooms and bathroom were on the second floor, we had to set up a space downstairs for mom.

At this point my sister made arrangements to come home and stay with mom and dad. She had three to possibly four weeks she could offer. Having worked in the medical field, and just being a natural at patient care, this was a relief for me as I was not. I am so the opposite; I can sit with and be there, but doing actual patient care was not in my skill set. This was another thing mom and I shared. When her mom was needing care at home prior to going to a nursing home, mom would go and do her best, but she struggled and shared her stories with me.

I step back here for a moment. January of this year my sister's daughter was married in Kentucky where they now lived. It was a blessing that we as a family, mom and dad, mom's sister, our cousin, were all able to go and celebrate this together. Little did we know it would be a last time.

Also prior to this, David and I had planned a vacation, the first in a very long time with just the two of us. We were going to take two weeks and just drive US Highway 12 from our town to the west coast.

Back to July. David and I wanted to cancel our trip so we would be available to help out, but mom insisted that we go. Sandy was there and she would be fine. Near the end of July David and I set out on our trip, with mixed emotions. We kept in touch with my sister everyday checking on how mom was doing. By the beginning of the second week, Sandy said mom seemed to be slipping and we might want to consider coming home. We modified our route and headed home. We were able to spend some time with mom and showed her pictures from the trip which she appreciated but soon thereafter she was slipping into longer periods of sleep.

My final day with mom was a Sunday. She was not awake all that much. Hospice had been called in and were treating her with comfort measures. I had a migraine headache festering all day and by evening, feeling there was nothing more we could do we headed home. Two hours later Sandy called to let us know mom had gone home to Jesus. I asked Sandy if she had seen the light of Jesus coming for mom. As I had with grandma I so wanted to be there when mom passed, just for one more chance to see Jesus come. That I was not frustrated me, but my sister did share that mom said she saw the light coming for her from the front of the house. That was a great comfort for me.

The passing of any parent is hard, but when it is your mother, it is different and harder, and so it was for me. You know it is coming, but until it does, it is not really real.

As my sister's available time was limited, the week was full. Not only the funeral arrangements but there was dad, how we were going to care for him, and what and where that was going to look like and be. Together we visited options and did our best to make decisions, but a lot of ends had to be tied up. Three days after the funeral my sister had to return home, and it was now on David and me to finalize all things.

My dad, unlike David's dad when his mom died, was not able to live alone in their home. It simply was more than he could handle. He no longer drove a car, and he had depended on mom for so many things. Mentally he was ok, and physically he was not ill, just old. We knew we would have to sell their home of fifty-eight years, and it sold quickly. Within five weeks of mom's passing, we had dad packed up and moved into a senior apartment complex just two blocks from our home. We only moved what he would need, along with some comforts of home and memory for him. Dad could join other seniors for activities and one main meal each day.

He was able to fix breakfast and a light supper, do his laundry, and take care of the apartment. David did his grocery shopping and we took him to appointments as needed.

My sister came home again from Kentucky after dad was moved to help me finish going through our parents' home. Prior to dad moving, I went to the house every day after work to tackle going through all of mom's things. Dad had no interest in helping me so it all fell on me. Cleaning out from the attic to the basement and through the garage, we found things that not only dated back to our childhood, but our parents' childhood. The volume of decisions to make in a ten-day period was almost insurmountable. We had family come in to take or buy what they might want, which helped, but so much was left. Neither my sister or I had space or room for much of it. I packed what I could to move to our basement to go through later, but much of it just went to the curb. We simply did not have time on our side as we had the closing on the house.

In less than two months, my mom died, our family home was empty, sold, no longer ours, and David and I acquired the responsibility of caring for my dad. David handled all the paperwork from mom's death, burial, and medical bills, to investment from the sale of the house, to insurance, Medicare, and dad's daily finances. It was a fast-tracked education on financially caring for a parent.

But financial was not the only fast track education we received. You think you know your parents, but until they become your full responsibility, you do not really know your parents. Just going through the few months of mom's battle with cancer, I saw sides of my dad that took me by surprise. To this day I wonder what their life was really like? I saw one thing, but there was much I did not. Just before my mom passed, she asked me, "Who is going to take care of your dad when I am gone?" I simply (naively) said, "David and I will." In my mind, was there any question, he certainly would not move to Kentucky with my sister. I so remember my mother's reply to me. She took my hand and squeezed hard and just said, "Oh Carol, oh Carol."

It didn't take long for the meaning of her words to come to fruition. Things that I saw hints of became a reality. Dad just transferred everything he had expected or received from mom, to me. He called me constantly, whether at home or work or driving between, he wanted this, needed that, come now to do this. I left home by six in the morning and returned home close to five in the evening, after working a full day with overtime. David had much the same schedule, and it became clear, really fast that some boundaries had to be established. I was so emotionally pressed that it was David who stepped up. We talked to dad and laid out the rules. Just like raising your children, it takes a bit for them to learn, abide by, and live in the boundaries, and so it was with dad. Eventually we arrived at the mutually acceptable middle.

The six months of transition were stressful and all of my stress settled in my weakest place, my back and sciatic. The pain was so bad that standing, sitting, laying all hurt. I was on a large amount of pain relievers, and they failed to touch the pain. My doctor said I was experiencing situational depression and wanted to put me on medication for it, along with the pain relievers. I refused and took the bull by the horns and gained control over my stress and my pain through basic breathing, yoga, exercise, and a lot of leaning on the Lord and giving it up to Him. David was, though frustrated, so helpful, kind, loving, understanding, and protective.

It was about this time that our son came to us with the news that his marriage was in trouble and they had separated. I felt my heart breaking in ways it never had before. My son was hurting and I never knew pain such as this in my heart ever. Nothing is so helpless as seeing your child hurting, wanting desperately to fix it and make it better, and there is nothing you can do to make that happen. Your arms ache to hold him, comfort him, but what he needs is your ear to listen, the assurance of your love, the knowledge that your door is always open, no judgment, and your prayers. That we could give him.

The next few years taught us how to navigate our way around emotional, relational, and family changes that were not smooth, straight, or expected. Our son moved home for a short while as he worked through the dynamics of divorce, reestablishing his independence, and finding a new place to live.

CHAPTER 18

More Changes

Perspective: new job, family, and health issues. Our move to the new home that split the time of the drive—shorter for David, longer for me—was a good move, until it was not. David had worked for many startup companies, in the same industry, and with some of the same coworkers. Each move was a better, stronger move. But this time was different. The business was in trouble and David knew he had to leave before bad turned to worse. David landed a job that was three hours north of where we now were living, and you guessed it, we were planning to move again. We had our house on the market and were looking for a new home to buy in the new city. In addition to job changes and house selling/hunting, we had to research a place for dad as he would be moving with us. School had let out for the summer, so I also began job hunting. Meanwhile, David drove up north on Sunday, back home on Friday, staying in an apartment during the week. We did this for two and a half months. I had actually landed a new job, and started working. Since the house had not sold, I did not quit my job at the school until the last minute, giving a two-week notice.

Before my two weeks were up, David had just had it with the travel and not a single prospect of selling our house. The prospect of not knowing when we could move, all this driving, just made it all feel wrong. He left his job, and I left my new job and asked my principal if I could keep my job at the school. He was pleased to keep me on. One might ask, what are you thinking? Well, David was known in his industry and had contacts. Within three weeks, he had a new job. The project he would be working on was in Switzerland. When he was not working in Switzerland, he was working in his office at home. His new schedule was two weeks gone, two weeks home, and this was our life for the next nine months. It may seem odd that this was actually better, but it was. We did not have to move, dad did not have to be moved, I kept my job, David liked the work and the people, and he enjoyed Switzerland.

Working in Switzerland was in and of itself an adventure. Weekends David and coworkers would get on the train and explore, mostly Switzerland, but they had opportunities to see on a smaller scale, parts of France and Germany. With his superior abilities to navigate, David would map out a route and they would take in the sites the countries had to offer. Camera in hand, David took many pictures to share and remember his experiences.

As big as the adventure of working in Europe was, David had another personal road of adventure to travel, one that would last longer and become a significant part of his life going forward. Because of David's significant health issues, our doctor wrote a letter to the courts to have David's adoption records opened. David was adopted just four months after his birth. The court was helpful and promptly got his records opened. We did not gain a lot of beneficial health information from his birth mother, and his birth father was not listed, other than the statement that he had "significant health issues." A whole new door was about to open, bringing new families in our lives.

The records revealed enough information for David to start looking for his birth family as another possible source of information. The door to finding his "roots" was slowly opening. His research, DNA testing, working with Ancestry, 23andMe, and other resources has aided him in locating some of his birth family information and history, ultimately leading to meeting some of his birth family members. Because of his own search and enjoyment of the process, David expanded his efforts to creating family trees, of his birth family, his adoptive family, and my family, as well as assisting others in finding their roots. Finding your roots, learning family history, is an amazing journey and has become a passion in our lives.

But the road on this journey had another bump, curve, and unexpected twist. It was a routine morning, but I noticed David's legs below his knees appeared to be very bruised. I asked him what happened, and he said, "Yeah, I noticed it too and thought I might call the doctor." A strong conversation ensued, and David was agreeing to call the doctor before I left for work. The day took a bit of a twist. After seeing the second doctor, David came to see me at school. He was bleeding internally and was to report to the hospital in Madison right away. But David being David said, I have to clean up a couple of things for work at home first. We both drove home, called our son Austin to come, and by the time he arrived we were packed and on our way to the hospital. Once in the hospital treatment began immediately. As they brought in the first transfusion, they told him this was the cost of a new car. Thus, began ten months of treatment, healing and change.

In the course of ruling out and narrowing down the cause of platelet loss the doctors also tested for, yes, the big "C," cancer. I recall sitting in a waiting room while a spinal tap was to be done, and this paralyzing wave of fear came over me. The fear of cancer, of David going through pain, and dying. I closed my eyes and started praying as the fear nearly choked the air out of me. I knew God was in control, and whatever lay ahead He would be right there walking us through it, but in the moment, I was fearful. As God urged me to breathe in Jesus, and exhale fear, while reminding me of a verse:

For God has not given us a spirit of fear and timidity, but of power, love, and self-discipline. (2 Timothy 1:7 NLT)

A nurse interrupted me, asking if I would like to go into the room with David. It was like a weight being lifted off my heart, and I said, "Could I? Yes!" They explained to me that they had given David a drug where he was awake, could talk, but would not feel pain. The not so often seen side of David had kicked in and his humor was the very medicine I needed in that moment, and I was comforted by the Spirit of God in me, assuring me that all was well.

David did not have cancer, he had a condition, ITP (formerly known as idiopathic), and now known as (immune thrombocytopenic purpura), a disorder that can lead to easy or excessive bruising and bleeding. The bleeding results from unusually low levels of platelets, the cells that help blood clot. David's platelet count was very low.

Over the coming months, David had regular IV and steroid treatments to increase his platelet count. It was physically exhausting for him and interrupted his awake and sleeping schedule big time. He was able to do some work from home, which increased as time went on. Through this whole experience God was watching over us, providing for use, and, most importantly, answering the prayers for healing. We praised God for good health insurance that covered all but a small portion of the cost.

David did recover, and though it could return, it has not. It did leave him with insulin dependent diabetes, and he previously was diagnosed as a type II diabetic and was being treated with oral medication that controlled it. By God's grace, David takes these things in stride, but for me they prove to be bigger bumps in the road. It has been a learning process for both of us, and with the help of wonderful doctors, we have navigated the change well.

CHAPTER 19

Grandparents, Funerals, Switzerland

Perspective: grandparents, funerals, Switzerland again. One of life's greatest joys brought another change. Born into our lives, we became grandparents to our beautiful granddaughter, Emma Rose. She arrived in July, and I was able to go and be in the hospital the night Emma was born and the subsequent week at their home. By the weekend David traveled down as did Emma's Uncle Austin. Within about a year or shortly thereafter, Kevin and Amiee moved to Wisconsin and lived a short hour and a half away. It was such a joy to be able to just drive up and see them all and watch how Emma changed and grew. They started out in an apartment and soon moved into a home.

It was not long after we felt like things were settling that David's dad's health took a turn with a diagnosis of cancer, so once again, we were helping to move him from his home to an assisted living facility where he would receive the care he needed. Having a brother living near dad eased the burden of care. David's brother took the lead on handling things and we supported where we could. It was hard to watch dad decline. He had been so active in his lifetime, pastoring multiple churches, being on dart ball teams, golfing, and enjoying the fellowship of parishioners. He was an educated and informed man, so watching the decline mentally was hard. It was not long before we were attending the funeral of another parent and going through the final business of taking a lifetime and a home apart.

Shortly thereafter, my father contracted a MRSA infection on his knees where he had replacements done years earlier which involved surgery, rehab, and a move to a nursing home facility. This move was emotional as it was the final process of taking their home apart. Dad settled into the nursing home routine and was content to be taken care of, though he struggled with some rules and living with a roommate. He enjoyed the attention of staff and the social life provided.

David had joined with a friend and business associate to establish a new company creating a service to the industry they had worked in for many years. It was an exciting and challenging new opportunity for them, and it was not long before they were back on the project previously worked on in Switzerland. David loved Switzerland and was excited to be going back. He spent ten months traveling, three weeks in Switzerland, ten days home.

His travels coincided with my dad's stay in the nursing home. Christmas had come and gone, and things seemed to be settling down. All reports from the staffing's with dad were good, and it felt like we were moving quietly into the new year. Early January we received a call from the nursing home asking us to come in and meet with dad and the social worker. Dad was refusing to take some medications, and a family meeting to make changes was required. Now dad was still in charge of his choices, but the family had to be on board. After explaining to Dad and us the ramifications of not taking some medications, and David reiterated this with dad to make sure he understood the choice he was making, it was approved.

It was a Friday, end of January that David returned to Switzerland. Just previous to this trip the nursing home said they would be calling Hospice in to give dad some extra care and attention. We questioned why, but it seemed to be normal procedure. Sunday morning, I received a call from the nursing home stating that I should come as they did not think he would live through the day. I was taken back by this news as he had seemed good just a few days prior. I called Austin to see if he was available to join me, and he arrived early afternoon. Dad had been sleeping and did not wake up. I talked to him, sang some of his favorite songs, and with no change Austin and I left around 6:00 pm. The phone rang about 1:00 am and it was the nursing home informing me that my dad had passed. I guess dad had just decided enough was enough, and he was ready to go to Jesus and join mom.

I called David in Switzerland, and he made arrangements to come back home. Having handled everything for him since mom had died, David just knew what needed to be done and we got it done. My sister was called, arrangements made, and we were putting to rest the last of our earthly parents. It was a small, just family funeral at the funeral home. We sent dad off with his favorite hymn, "Wonderful Grace of Jesus." There was a quiet snowfall at the cemetery covering us with the peace of God.

CHAPTER 20

Reminiscing

Perspective: reminiscing. When you have buried your parents, gone through their years of memories, treasures, and just everyday life, you fast find yourself asking questions. Photo albums initiate many questions. Presumably they are pictures of family members and friends that perhaps played an important role in their lives, but names and places were missing, and even the few that were there did not always connect with our memory.

As you sort through things and find a place for each item, you wonder if you have done the right thing. Did this have special meaning or purpose? Should it be kept in the family, or even given to someone who may have shared in the memory? You are always constrained by time to empty out a household, so you make your best guess, pack up what you think should have closer attention, and stack piles of boxes in your own basement to be gone through, sometime. Sometime turns into many small visits to the boxes, whatever you can squeeze into your own busy schedule, life, and routine.

But those unanswered questions, they sit like a bad taste in your mouth, one that comes and goes but is never resolved. Why did we not talk about these things when mom and dad were alive and with us? Perhaps they did, but we were not paying attention, did not value the importance, and came during a quick holiday visit when many other things were on our plate. So much history, so much family, substance, things that made us who we are today. Gone.

Then one day, after you have sorted through boxes of stuff, disposed, given away, and retained, you get down to their certificates, journals, Bibles with notes in the margin, or pieces of papers slipped between the pages. You find records of expenditures they made, things they purchased, cards they exchanged, and letters they kept. The photos, the many photos. You find yourself slowing down, taking time, and getting lost in all thing's mom and dad. You recognize the handwriting, maybe a phrase they repeated often, and then, the faint, but ever so real, scent of their presence.

Flood gates open, in your mind, your heart, and your eyes. That lump in your throat swells to such an enormous size you can barely breathe. Where did the time go? Once, long ago, you thought your parents would just always be with you. Not being with you was not on the radar, and now realize that almost twenty years have passed since your first parent left this earth for heaven. You come to the realization that you, you, are now the oldest generation in your family, and it terrifies you. If you are fortunate enough to not be the oldest of your siblings, as is my case, you comfort yourself with the thought that there is a little buffer there. But even then, you realize, you both are older, and you begin to resent the distance of miles between you. You long to have your backyards border each other so that you, like you did once with your parents, do not waste the precious time you have together.

Then another reality hits you. Your own children, your grandchild, living miles away from you. You get together twice a year if you are lucky, and the visits are so full that before you know it, they are pulling out of your driveway to head home. Sometimes schedules interfere and you do not even have your own children, home, under the same roof, at the same time. Your heart pounds a little faster as the reality sets in, history repeating itself, right in front of your eyes.

Near the end of the ten months of David working in Switzerland, another health issue presented itself. David had developed a blood clot. Thankfully it was caught early and resolved, but the doctor grounded him from air travel. We had hoped to take a trip together to Switzerland as David wanted to show me around, but that was not going to happen. Having David around, functioning and healthy, for me was better than a trip to Switzerland. David would now be working out of his office in our home remotely, going into the office only two or three times a month. Over time some changes in personnel with his company put David into a position of more responsibility, and like any change of this nature, it had its positives and negatives. We choose to focus on the positives and it has worked well. We established a routine and schedule and life seemed to settle.

We enjoyed the years we had with Kevin, Amiee, and Emma close by. Frequent visits became part of our new routine. Emma had started school, played some soccer, and started ballet, and we were able to go and see these things she was involved in. Watching your granddaughter grow up has a bonus because it is all pleasure with none of the work and responsibility of being a parent. You can spoil with no regrets, play because you have time, but at the end of the day, hug, kiss, and go home to your own quiet house. We felt very blessed. Until when Emma was between nine and ten years old and the blessing developed a kink. Kevin's parents operate a multi-generational family farm and trucking business. As his dad was getting older, they asked if Kevin, Amiee, and Emma might move back to his home town to help out with planting and harvest. Giving some time to weigh the situation, a decision was made to make the move. They sold their home, packed up a lot of stuff, and during the summer made the move back to Kevin's home town. The move put them over five hours away from us, and it was hard to see them go. Our frequent visits were now, gone.

Life changed again, and as before, life continues forward.

CHAPTER 21

Living and Enjoying Life

Perspective: living and enjoying life. Between the death of David's dad and my dad, we were fortunate to make a dream become a reality. We have always loved cars, and even though we were confined to family cars most of our life together, we still made sure those family cars were sleek, stylish, and had a little get up and go under the hood.

David had a Z28 Camaro when we met, but this time we were shopping for a Corvette. We spent the better part of nine months talking to sales people, checking out features, colors, and all things important to our decision to purchase. We came upon a well-seasoned car dealer Corvette enthusiast with whom David felt comfortable and who since became a good friend. The day came when we flew to Nashville, rented a car and drove to Bowling Green, Kentucky, to the Corvette Museum to do a museum pickup of our 2011, Inferno Orange, Grand Sport Corvette.

With the museum pickup, we had a personal tour of the Corvette plant where they are made. David was given the opportunity to drive one off the assembly line and given a birth certificate for the car for doing so. After a lunch with our personal guide for the day, we went onto the showroom floor where he spent about three hours going over every single detail of the car. We received a plaque and certificates, and after everything was signed, I rode in the car as our guide drove it down a long hallway lined with employee well-wishers, clapping their hands and shouting congratulations to us. David was waiting just at the end as we pulled out into the sunshine. The car was stunning!

The next morning, we started our journey home in our new Corvette, and it has delivered fun, new friends, great trips, and memories, in addition to making us feel much younger than reality, ever since. Living in Wisconsin, with snow, ice, salt and sand during the winter months, the Corvette is a fair-weather friend, used between the months of April and if we are lucky into November. Remarkably, of our three vehicles, the Corvette is not only the most comfortable, but delivers the best gas mileage. Yes, it only seats two people, but we consider it our "dating" car, and seating for two is perfect!

Having a Corvette presented us with new opportunities. Car enthusiast enjoy car events, road rallies, car shows, car racing, and fundraising for important causes. Joining a Corvette Club helped to facilitate availability to these events. The most frequent of the major fundraising was St. Jude Peoria to Memphis Corvette Drive fundraiser. Drivers and passenger raise a minimum of $1,500 that is donated directly to St. Jude's Children's Research Hospital. Leaving from Peoria, Illinois, a line of Corvettes with a police escort drive to Memphis, Tennessee. A day is spent at St. Jude's starting with a breakfast and overview of the work being done at St. Jude's and then a tour of the facility, ending with children and families coming out to meet drivers, sit in the Corvettes, and photo opportunities. David has gone on the drive two times. I accompanied him on the first trip, our son went the second time. It truly is amazing to witness firsthand the miracles happening each day in the lives of children with cancer.

We also have worked a Corvette event for a number of years called Corvette Adventures. David and I assist another couple who really do the bulk of the planning, organizing, and publicity. There are three events each year, the largest being in June with two smaller ones in September. We have enjoyed the time, made many new friends, and seen some awesome cars, and the work is fun, sometimes despite the weather.

Twice we participated in the Corvette Caravan, a nationwide event where Corvettes travel in groups to the birth place of all Corvettes, Bowling Green, Kentucky. Both times David was the co-captain for the North Central Group where he would lead the caravan that at times had upwards of 750 Corvettes following him on the Interstate. The Caravan happens every five years, and the five years in-between are spent coordinating and organizing groups. Our last caravan (and we were only one of many caravans) had cars from Alaska, Canada, Hawaii, and states from the Pacific Ocean to Wisconsin, as well as a friend of ours from France. By the time everyone has arrived in Bowling Green, you can easily witness over 7,000 Corvettes all together in one place. What better company could you ask for as you sit in the traffic jam!

We took three other significant trips, one to Black Hills Gold in South Dakota with a small group of Corvette enthusiast friends, one to Tennessee for The Tail of the Dragon and on to Ashville, North Carolina, to the Biltmore Estate with a group sponsored by the National Corvette Museum, and one to Niagara Falls, just the two of us. Of course, any fair-weather travel to see our daughter's family or my sister, are in the Corvette. Most of our pleasure comes when we just take a drive after work or on weekends. As when we were dating, we still enjoy exploring the back roads to nowhere and the beauty we find along the way. Weather permitting, the roof is off, and there simply is no better way to relax.

CHAPTER 22

Moving Again

Perspective: moving again. As I approached the age of sixty-five, kicking and screaming I might add, we came to realize that some major decisions for our life lay just ahead on the horizon. I loved my job, and I could not ask for a better boss, and these two factors alone put the thoughts of retirement on the back burner. I had honestly thought I would just work another six years, until I was seventy, and then it would probably be time to consider retirement. David being the practical, forward-looking planner in the family began posing questions that realistically demanded answers. He said we need to start planning now, and the first thing we need to do is move to a house where everything is on one floor. Since before I was a teenager, I have dealt with sciatica, and learned to manage life with it. Our home was a two-story home, with bedrooms upstairs and a first-floor laundry. Stair steps, though still doable, were becoming more challenging.

With both of us still working, the time was now. David's focus was to make my forty-five-minute drive to work, shorter as he worked from home. My daily schedule had me rising at 4:30 am, leaving home by 6:00 am, starting work at 6:45 am and working until 4:00 pm and arriving home at 4:45 pm and to bed by 8:00 pm.

My days were busy, multitasking was my job description. I rarely took a lunch away from my desk, and breaks were just quick trips to the restroom. My weekends were scheduled with laundry, house and yard work, cooking, church, and a little down time if I could squeeze it in.

This goal marked the area of our search. We were open to what we could find, but our preference was, new, open concept, three-car garage, washer and dryer would fit, and I kind of wanted white woodwork and kitchen cabinets. We put into God's hands and asked for His guidance and clarity in making decisions.

Though we had without success tried to sell our house before, we took that leap of faith and put it on the market to get the ball rolling. I began searching houses for sale. Working with our Relator, I gave him lists, and he set up appointments. We would find a house, I would fall in love, and it would be sold just like that. Then one day I happened upon a new build, just went on the market, and we had an appointment to go see it. I loved it. We measured the very large two car garage and determined that with careful planning, we could get all three cars in the garage. The washer and dryer would fit, it was open concept, and the woodwork and cabinets were white. Bedrooms had carpet, bathrooms tile, and hardwood floors for the rest. Perfect. This house had more closet space that we had ever had, two sinks in the master bath (first time ever) and a walk-in shower like we wanted. We called our son to come with us for a second look, and during this visit we discovered the neighbor had, yes, a Corvette!

We made an offer, it was accepted, and we had an offer on our house also. Getting to closing, working through all the detailed paperwork, proved to be a bit stressful. But each time an obstacle presented itself, we prayed, and God creatively made the path straight. The closing time frames coordinated perfect for both houses, and before we knew it, I was packing us up for our thirteenth move. We had purchased our kitchen appliances, and got

Black Friday pricing on them! Moving day, in November, it was sunny and in the seventies. There were endless small but significant ways God steered us through this move. His hand in every detail was so evident, and our hearts were grateful, and at peace. My drive to work was now only fifteen minutes, and not on county roads, but a four-lane state highway.

We moved less than one week before Thanksgiving. The stove and refrigerator came just before Thanksgiving, and the microwave and dishwasher the weekend after. My sister and her husband came for Thanksgiving. We had a great time unpacking, putting things away, cooking turkey and putting up the Christmas tree. My first drive to work was sweet. It seemed I had just left home and I was pulling into the parking lot. Truly a blessing.

CHAPTER 23

Noteworthy

Perspective: noteworthy. The biggest asset I have is David. To say that I am one very spoiled lady is an understatement, but it is my story and I am sticking to it. Granted, it was not always that way back in the early days of marriage, but once I let go of the reins and allowed David to be the head of the home God created him to be, truly, I reaped the rewards of God's best blessings.

Working from home David would just handle things as he had time. Some laundry here, vacuum a room there, load and unload the dishwasher, always mowed the lawn, cleared the snow, took care of the garbage, and, for which I am eternally grateful, made the grocery list, clipped the coupons, did the grocery shopping, brought it home, and put it away. Did I mention, I hate grocery shopping. When David was traveling to Switzerland, he made sure the shelves and freezer were stocked before he left. A few times I had to grocery shop. I started when we were first married because I just thought it was my job. It would take me three hours or more just at the store, not to mention all that list making, coupon clipping, and storing it away. Of course, do not forget, loading and unloading the car.

Now I can already hear some of you say, I hear you sister, what is your secret? Simple, David absolutely loves grocery shopping. He even bags his own when given the opportunity. Having worked in a grocery store in high school, he learned the stocking, moving, sales, and process of getting it from shelf to out the door "game" as he put it and finds it challenging each time he crosses the threshold of the "grocery store." Whenever we have moved, before settling on a location, David scouts out the grocery shopping opportunities and decides if he approves or not. Destinations have been eliminated on this research alone. And God gave this man, to me! I am so blessed!

It is not that I never go to the grocery store, but only when I really "have" to. One of those "have to" trips turned into one of my lesser joyous adventures. It occurred when David had hernia surgery. Nothing too serious, but lift restrictions enforced. No, he did not send me to the grocery store, but he did take me with him, you know, to lift and stretch. He pushed the cart and sent me on the food gathering missions. Remember, I rarely darken the door of a grocery store, and admittedly, my knowledge of the place is limited. So off he sends me to get the best head of lettuce, be sure it is firm. I am leaning in, reaching far and wide, testing each head, after all, I did not want to fail my assignment. I heard a sound that resembled thunder but made nothing of it until the sprinkler started showering the lettuce, and me along with it. My next assignment was something that just happened to be on the top shelf. David had moved on with the cart, but did manage to glance back when he heard things falling on the floor. I was too short, and in my stretch and reach, my coat caught items on the lower shelves, depositing them on the floor. I cleaned up my mess. The final challenge of this particular trip was the retrieving of items off a bottom shelf, and not just one, but multiples. Reaching in to complete my task, as quickly as I could, without paying close attention, I smacked my head on the shelf and landed on my back side on the floor. David could no longer restrain his laugh, as he walked on down the aisle as if he never knew me.

Now, I will accompany David to the grocery store, just as an outing with him. When not forced to do the actually shopping, the grocery store is a fascinating place. So many things I never even knew existed, just sitting there on the shelf smiling at me. Before you know it, I am in the aisle alone, David is nowhere to be found, and I spend the next ten minutes searching up and down the aisles for him. Unfortunately, the grocery store is not the only place this happens. Pick a store, any store, or the County Fair, I am sure to be the one on my phone texting to David, "Where are you," only to hear my text being delivered to his phone nearby. Somehow, though I am wandering he manages to keep track of me, and yes, even amusing himself at my expense by following me to see how long it takes me to locate him.

Additionally, I was not gifted with a good sense of direction. The many times we go for rides, it does not take long for me to get lost. It is just easier to enjoy the ride and not worry about where we are, that's David's job after all. When giving me directions, do not use words like "east, west, north, and south." My world is left, right and straight ahead. But even better than left and right, is "the big red barn" or the "purple house." Give me actual landmarks and I am happy. Knowing this, never, and I mean never, divert me off a known course in the dark, or for that matter, fog, snow, or rain. Lost will be my demise. Yes, cars today have navigation, and mine does. It even will talk to me if I ask. The particular multitasking skill of watching a map and the road, does not work for me, period. I can only concentrate on one thing at a time, the road, or the map. To use the map, I would need to pull off and study it. Then there is the talking lady. We do not have a good relationship. Even when David occasionally uses her, I argue with her, and I win! I will give her this, she is polite and does not argue back. Driving on multiple lanes in big cities terrifies me, and I only do it if there is absolutely no alternative. But I prepare for such excursions by having David prepare written directions well in advance for me to study. Luckily, he knows exactly what I need. A friend once described riding with me as being more fun than shopping, and she was a shopper. It has also been suggested that if I am allowed off on my own, be sure I have plenty of gas, and a way to purchase more.

Parking lots are challenging also. After I park the car and before heading inside, I turn around as if I am coming out and take special note of exactly where I parked. I always try to park strategically in accordance to my natural tendencies, being the creature of habit I am. There was a time in our lives where we both worked but had only one car. David would always pick me up from work, and he always parked in the same place. However, one day someone else parked there and David was several stalls away. The car was the same color as ours (though not the same make or model). I confidently came out of the door, went to the car, got in, and said to the man in the car, "You are not my husband!" Immediately got out and found David a few stalls away with a big smile on his face. Well, someone has to keep life interesting, right!

CHAPTER 24

A Few Repairs

Perspective: a few repairs. The first summer after moving into our home, while we were at Corvette Adventures in June, David being the sprightly person he thought he was, fell in the road while running in a hurry to do something. I only point this out now because six months later, while attempting to clear snow from the driveway, he slipped and fell yet again. This time though, it hurt his shoulder, and David is not one to complain. A visit to the doctor determined he needed rotator cuff surgery, and it was scheduled for early January. It was challenging, but David soldiered through and met each of his recovery goals sooner than expected.

Then came the eye doctor appointment in July when I was told I would need cataract surgery, on both eyes. This news came about seven years sooner than I had originally been told. To put this in perspective, I had not had any major thing health wise since the birth of our son, over thirty-nine years ago. I truly had no idea what to expect. Insurance is always tricky, and this one was frustrating. My first surgeon had me scheduled for surgery to be completed on both eyes by the end of August, perfect timing for the start of school. Two days before surgery, we received a call that this surgeon was not on the approved list for insurance. We called the insurance company, they referred us to another surgeon, and I went through all the prep appointments again. Surgery was scheduled for October. Two days before surgery, a phone call, though the insurance company had her paperwork it had not yet been processed, and she was not approved. In this same clinic there was another surgeon who, after double checking, was approved. Once again, I went through the pre-surgery appointments and the first one was scheduled for just before Thanksgiving, and the second one, a week before Christmas.

What I imagined the surgery to be like, was not at all the reality. My anxiety was off the charts, and I was given the appropriate medication to settle me down. I remember praying so hard, and as I entered the operating room, all I could think of was seeing this on television, people went in alive and came out dead! Well, God is so good. His Spirit blanketed me with warmth and peace. Knowing what to expect, the second one was much easier. The results are wonderful. My ability to see so improved, and I no longer need glasses, well, except just to read.

My eyes were not the only thing that needed repair. Along about the same time as I received the news of my eyes, I developed this snapping in three of my fingers. An appointment with the doctor confirmed that I not only had two trigger fingers and one trigger thumb, I also had a condition called Dupuytren's contracture on two fingers. The eye surgeries had been scheduled and allowing enough time for complete recovery we scheduled these two surgeries for February, two weeks apart. These two surgeries went well, because as I expected I was completely out, and fortunately for me I had no pain. They looked gross, seeing them made me woozy, and stitch removal was the worst. My therapy went quicker than expected, and I creatively managed to accomplish things for the few weeks of healing and restrictions.

Though this year of surgeries, repairs, rehab, and therapy was unexpected, we came through it quite well. We both had the opportunity to care for each other in unaccustomed ways. At times our vulnerabilities showed their face, allowing us a better understanding of each other. One's strength was the other's courage. How precious, after forty-six years together, to learn new ways to love, and allow to be loved. God's work of making two into one is never ending.

CHAPTER 25

Decision to Retire

Perspective: making the decision to retire. We continued checking things off the preretirement list and started getting a feel for things. It is a lot to learn, and God equipped David with the ability to decipher and discern.

As significant as the eye surgery was in my life, just before the first surgery, a very good friend of over fifty years was diagnosed with pancreatic cancer and within the month went on to be with Jesus in early November. I could write pages on the role she played in my life, starting as early as when I was in high school. To draw a connection, she and her husband were the friends in Colorado that helped us through the purchase of the Christian bookstore and setting up the business, and this is just one of the many occasions of influence in our lives. Her passing, though great joy for her as Jesus welcomed her home, was a great loss to me. Ironically, she was just getting ready to retire.

It was wonderful to have the trigger fingers repaired. But again, with this personal triumph came another personal loss. Another dear friend, about to retire in just a little over two months, suffered a heart attack while getting ready for church on Sunday morning in February, and went to be with Jesus shortly thereafter. Our children grew up together. Our families connected for close to forty years. We share so many memories. She had one of those faces that smiled even if she was not actually smiling, her positive attitude could change the mood of a room, and her spirit was inspiring. Though meeting Jesus was her joy, it, again, was such a loss for me.

Come March I turned sixty-seven. Now my retirement plan was still to work for three more years. As mentioned, I loved my job, my boss was awesome, a brother in the Lord, and things at work were really good. Was it the four surgeries in four months or the loss of two very close and dear friends at or near my own age? Was I physically tired, emotionally drained, or a combination of all?

David and I had some serious conversations. He went over the financial consequences, evaluated where we were at, if we could afford it, and guessed as best we could what the future might look like if I should actually retire. We prayed over this major life-changing decision and by April, found real peace from God in saying yes to my retiring. But when, a date needed to be determined, I talked it over with my boss so that we could have the best scenario for the transition for him as well as the staff and school. No one else in our building did my job so training a replacement needed to be as thorough as possible. The great thing about a brother in the Lord as your boss, we prayed together over this decision and God lead us to picking June 30 as my retirement date.

A great deal of prayer, many conversations, and the gift of wisdom and discernment went into the hiring of my replacement. Where we started out was not where God had us end. God had a plan. He knew the outcome; we just had to listen, watch, and obey. The real bonus to my replacement was her twenty years of being an elementary school administrative assistant. Her experience and knowledge alone facilitated a smooth transition.

The last few months of school, and working were, to say the least, very busy. In addition to the normal end of year demands, I had to clean house. Sorting through eighteen plus years of changes, procedures, eliminate what was no longer applicable, and prepare what was needed to move forward. Desiring to make this transition smooth I set things up for months in advance, allowing my replacement the freedom of time to just settle into the routine, and the opportunity to get to know staff and families. I knew she was capable, but I did not want her overwhelmed. Accommodating a fresh start with a solid foundation would ensure a successful transition for the future.

The first "pinch me, this is real" had come the day the student body gathered for a surprise sendoff "thank you" celebration, confetti and all. Children have a way of making you feel like some sort of hero, but I just did not see myself that way. In an elementary school, to me at least, the true heroes, those who influence the most and will be remembered the longest, are the teachers. I was blessed to work with some awesome educators. In addition to them are all the wonderful support staff, instructional aides, para-professionals, counselors, nurse, nutrition department cooks and helpers, maintenance, and administration. They, to me, were the heart and soul of our school, and I had the high honor of serving them.

A few weeks after school had let out my wonderful staff took David and me out to dinner. The fellowship around the table was wonderful. Memories shared, gifts given, and then the one special treasure I will always cherish. My art teacher painted a picture of the ocean, sky, beach and orange flip-flops on the sand. It was beautiful, but further explanation revealed that each ripple in the ocean was the finger print of every student. Its home is on the mantle above the fireplace.

It had not yet set in, but I was going to miss this family and gathering of friends every day. In addition to them, were the children and their families. Each family, for the most part, spent six years in my building. Friendships are formed, connections made. Many came and went, but when a chance meeting in public happens, memories flood back, that is, of course, once I have figured out who they are. No person grows and changes more than when elementary children become adults. I look pretty much the same, and I was only one person to remember. I had close to five hundred children each year to acquaint myself with, together with their families. I have fast gotten over the embarrassment of asking for a name. This community that was mine every day, I was leaving behind.

June 30 came. My last day. When it finally arrived, it felt like a death in the family. My wonderful boss came. Together we prayed, hugged, and I turned in the keys that had given me admittance to this world for over eighteen years. We walked out together to our cars and left. Realistically, I knew I would see him, and for that matter, most everyone again, but in that moment, I was overcome by the feeling of separation, loneliness, and loss.

…retirement.

CHAPTER 26

Life Change

Perspective: life change. I drove home that day with a sense of loss. I did not know then just how great this loss would feel. The perspective of retirement is one of joy, freedom, spread your wings and fly. It would take time for that to become my reality, and I had no idea how long that might take. Once again, life change, no instruction manual. Like everything in life, I had not mapped out the big "plan." I have always sought God's direction for my life, the paths down which I would go, and retirement to me was no different. "Well, I am here God, what is next?"

The feeling of separation was enlarged by this policy. So not to compromise in anyway your retirement, you should not enter the school until after seventy days had passed. Though I am not much for rules that seemed dumb, I did comply with this one. I left my school in June and did not return again until mid-September.

I remember the first day I just popped back in for a quick visit. It was around the lunch hour and I popped into the lunchroom. I could never have anticipated what happened. Students all jumped up from their tables, called out my name, and surrounded me with the biggest group hug I have ever had. I had tears in my eyes. I had just worked in the office. My student contact was limited. But here, children mobbed me like I was the next best thing to chocolate. It took my breath away, I was speechless, all I could do was hug them. From there I went out on the playground to see some staff, and it happened again with the students.

I learned something very important that day. Never underestimate the influence one life, and in this case, my life, can make upon others. I would never have anticipated this response from the students, and the warmth of this reception will be in my memory forever.

CHAPTER 27

Where Am I Now?

Perspective: where am I now? It is the middle of February. Still cold and snowy outside. Just seven and a half months into retirement. These pages have recorded the journey of my life.

I am pleased to report, I am "beginning" to adjust to this new season in life. I was reminded just this week of how I miss the people I served, daily challenges, seeing God work in and through situations, lives, and daily routines. But in the next breath, I was also reminded that I do not miss 4:30 am starts to my day, driving in snowy conditions, the stress of deadlines, and the clock running the show of my life like a constant hand pushing on my back. The list does not stop there. I have come to embrace, enjoy, and appreciate, time with David, lingering over my morning coffee while reading God's Words to me, being a prayer warrior, watching the birds at the feeder, snuggling with my dog, getting dressed after 8:30 in the morning, time to cook and try new recipes, keep my house clean, exercise, walks in the afternoon, meeting with sister's in the Lord to study the Bible and pray together, staying up late, sleeping in till six. Slowly this list gets longer.

Seasons of change bring with them their own demons to be slayed. That which brought me to the decision of retirement now dares to taunt me. Age, growing older, physically, mentally, the shortening of my days, the loss of health, independence, control, fears, be they real imagined, or unreasonable, and yes, death, of spouse, family and friends.

As if "retirement" signals the beginning of the end. So, Satan would have me believe.

I admit, I have wrestled with the demons, but they will not win. Oh, they will not stop their relentless attacks, I am sure. But sugar, watch out, I have gone to The Rock for my defense. God is on my side, no, He is my whole team, Commander and Chief, Leader into battle, Protector, Preserver, Redeemer, Savior and Friend. Truth be known, the demons try to do battle, but this war is already history, and spoiler, because of Jesus, we won!

I am learning to breathe deep and exhale long.

I will be the first to admit, I have not arrived. The corners of the pages in my "retirement manual" are not bent over. I have not passed the test. I am not even studying for the test. Why?

Perspective: retirement is a "beginning," a "new start," opportunities to embrace, people to meet, friends to make, places to see, things to learn and do, accomplishments to obtained, history to write!

For as long as God grants me breathe to breath, I have a life to live. A life that matters, counts, is important, and worthy. I am an image bearer of Almighty God, the child of a King, created by and for God. Until the day God calls me home, I have a mission, a journey, and a purpose.

Perspective: God knows what is next, and I will follow His lead. In peace, I rest, assured that "it is well, with my soul."

CHAPTER 28

Something Unexpected

Perspective: something unexpected. Up to this point I have looked back on my life journey that has brought me to where I am today, learning new rhythms in my first year of retirement. I actually thought that I was beginning to get the hang of things.

After the holidays I had a "to do" list that I launched right into. Every time I scratched one off the list, I felt so accomplished. I had energy, I was inspired, and I was ready to conquer the world. I had gotten back into my routine of exercising, and I was feeling pretty good.

Mid-February, feeling like nothing was out of reach, I decided my body was ready to accomplish more. I had some stiffness and resistance in my right leg that kept me from being able to sit cross-legged like I was used to doing. I figured it was because I had slacked off in my daily exercise routine for longer than I should have, so I had a goal. To sit cross-legged!

Feeling exceptionally limber one Saturday morning I started pushing myself. You know, no pain, no gain. I had it all figured out in my head. I had googled exercises to accomplish my goal, and I was off to the races.

After a good stretching work out, I was feeling pretty good and was so productive the rest of that day. Next day came, and things were still pretty good, but I did notice a bit of an ache, but hey, that was to be expected.

Now, if you remember, I have had issues with my back and sciatic since before I was a teenager. My parents had taken me to chiropractors, doctors, and some therapy to try and figure out why I was hurting. They said it had to do with my body growing and inflammation in the vertebrae of my back. They recommended that I not do strenuous things because it irritated the inflammation.

The only strenuous thing I did not do was physical education (gym class) through my last three years of high school. I was ok with that. I did not like gym so I had a study hall instead. Unfortunately, at least this is my opinion, the damage was already done. In my pre-teen years, I spent a lot of time on my grandma's farm and considered my abilities equal to any good farmer. I carried bales of hay, five-gallon pails of water, up the hill to the sheep. I cleaned barn, I had my own garden, I did everything I had a mind to do. Looking back, I know I forced myself to do things I probably should not have done.

The price had been a bad back for as long as I can remember. Do something strenuous, my back would snap and I would hardly be able to walk. Sometimes it took nothing more than changing the liner in a waste basket, or making a bed. For as long as I can remember, I experience back pain at night which would wake me up to change positions. I have applied ice and heat more times than I can count, and have taken my share of anti-inflammatory meds. I would always soldier through, doing a full rest for a day or two, but I had school, work, a family, things to do and responsibilities.

As I got older, I found that just stress alone would be enough to cause my back to go out. The worst bout of long-term sciatic pain from stress was right after my mom died and I had my dad to look after. It took six to eight months before I felt complete relief. But to this day, on many different levels and for many different reasons, I experience pain on my right lower back and down my right leg. It is my weak trigger spot.

Well, you can guess what happened by day three of my enthusiastic stretching in February. That is right, pain in my sciatic and down my right leg. It took almost a month for me to start feeling more like myself. After multiple lectures I realized, I might have to accept the fact that I might not sit cross-legged like I used to. I had suspended any aggressive exercise and was just focusing once again on stretches I had learned over the years for the healing process of a pinched sciatic nerve.

Mid-March I was feeling much improved. I had a doctor's appointment concerning a trigger thumb on my right hand on Wednesday, March 18, 2020. We were in the midst of the COVID-19 process of things shutting down. As it happened, the hospital was closing all elective surgery starting on Saturday, March 21, my birthday. My doctor said he would get me scheduled before that happened, so on Thursday, March 19, I was scheduled for surgery on my thumb. With the exception of the long wait, surgery scheduled for 1:45, actually happened at 4:45, all went well. Throughout the healing process and stitch removal I had no pain, well, in my thumb that is.

We were under this stay safe at home quarantine and life was a bit boring. We had a 1500-piece puzzle with pictures of pies that we decided we would amuse ourselves with and help to pass the confining indoor time as the weather was not all that agreeable for outdoor activity. We sort of celebrated my 68th birthday on Saturday. I was not doing much as my right hand had a large bandage from surgery. Come Sunday afternoon, I decided to do some serious puzzle-solving. David was finding pieces left and right, and then decided to quit. I on the other hand forged ahead, leaning over the table in search of many perfect pieces for well over two hours, despite suggestions that maybe I should stop, which of course I did not heed. Well, my mistake.

Monday morning, I woke to pain in my back, hip, and down my right leg. This was tear worthy pain. It hurt to stand, walk, sit, lay down. Nothing relieved the pain. I immediately started taking a double dose of Aleve and applied ice on my back. I attempted to lay down with my feet raised above my head, draw my knees in to stretch, but nothing helped. Come bedtime, no way could I lay in bed. I spent the night in the recliner with ice.

I soldiered through until Thursday when I finally listened to David and messaged the doctor. They got three prescriptions to the pharmacy, one was prednisone to reduce inflammation, one was a muscle relaxer and one was for pain. I started two of them on Thursday night and on Friday morning I was taking all three. Relief started coming, but it was slow. I had medicine for six days, and it was clear by day five, I needed them refilled. The same day of the refill I had my stitches removed from my thumb. Still, no pain from the thumb and it was healing remarkably well.

By the time the refills ran out I was well into week three and called for a refill again of the pain med and the muscle relaxer. As I entered week four, I started sleeping half the night in bed, half the night in the recliner. By week five I was actually able to walk outside again, and time spent in bed was longer, while time in recliner became less. I was still using ice and heat every day. Week six I felt good enough to clean the house, a little bit each day done carefully. By the weekend I felt it was well beyond time to put nail polish on my toes and get them flip flop worthy, a task I had hoped to have done before my birthday. I took three days to accomplish the task, doing it carefully. But, by Monday of week seven, I had a setback. This time just one day of annoying pain, but enough to cause me to take the strong meds which I had not completely used, and to spend the rest of the week taking it really easy. The weather was chilly so I was not walking either.

By the end of week seven I was off the strong meds, sleeping in bed all night, and starting to feel much improved. Week eight I did light housekeeping, all the laundry and cooking, a little yard work, and taking short walks. The weekend of week eight was our forty-fifth wedding anniversary. We took a two-hour ride in the Corvette, and I felt no pain the entire day. Beginning of week nine marked the finish of the puzzle which I joyfully took apart and put away. It was also the first time I drove my own car since December, and the first time I drove a car since middle of March.

It was now the middle of week ten. Two and a half months dealing with the second bout of pinched sciatic nerve. I was back to normal and off all strong pain medication, my daily activities were back to normal, I was taking slightly longer walks, and the pain was gone, though I still experience some normal achiness.

Something unexpected. Why did I share this experience? It came in the midst of being quarantined at home. Stores closed, churches closed, no hair appointment since February as salons and all small business were closed. We literally could do nothing and go nowhere, except for a ride in the car. I felt like I was under a double quarantine. What does any of this have to do with where I have been, how I got to this time in my life, or where I go in life from here.

Nothing happens without purpose. I cannot speak to the broad spectrum of God's purpose, but I can, to the personal experience of my purpose.

CHAPTER 29

Conviction, Confession, Surrender

Perspective: conviction, confession, surrender. It was the end of week two, beginning of week three. God spoke to me one morning through the following verse, a devotional, and through a comment made by daughter, Amiee this morning, after sharing with her that I actually slept 10 1/2 hours the night before.

Her comment: "Baby steps."

The verse: "But you, dear friends, carefully build yourselves up in this most holy faith by praying in the Holy Spirit, staying right at the center of God's love, keeping your arms open and outstretched, ready for the mercy of our Master, Jesus Christ. This is the unending life, the real life!" (Jude 1:20–21 MSG).

A devotional reading: It used very familiar verses that perfectly applied to me.

"My grace is sufficient for you, for My power is made perfect in weakness" (2 Corinthians 12:9 NIV).

The Bible doesn't provide specifics, but we are told that the apostle Paul struggled with what he called a "thorn in his flesh." Whatever the problem was, it bothered Paul and he pleaded with God three times to remove it, but God refused. Instead, God told Paul that His grace was sufficient and he needed to rely on God's power rather than his own. Kind of sounded like what I was doing, except I didn't ask God to fix it, or remove the reason I could not sit cross-legged.

But the next verse really hit home:

Do you not know that you are the temple of God and that the Spirit of God dwells in you? (1 Corinthians 3:16)

The Bible is full of important truths we tend to forget, and this is one of those for me. The Spirit is present to help me in my weaknesses. Not only was I in my own determined way trying to fix my body, get rid of the weakness that prevented me from sitting cross-legged, but I was totally ignoring the fact that my actual body is the temple of God, the place where the Holy Spirit dwells. The Holy Spirit helps, teaches, guides, convicts, and empowers us to glorify God. Did I even bother to consult God or ask for help in doing something to this "temple of God"? No. Every Christ's follower is a temple of the living God and is holy. Jesus knew we would need help which is why He gave us a Helper, the Holy Spirit. I was reminded that I need to be mindful of the Holy Spirit's presence and continually rely on His strength.

Two nights prior to this morning was an awful night of restlessness, no sleep, pain in my back, upset stomach, despair over this, and fear of old age, living the rest of my life with no relief from this sciatica, death, finishing weak, and failure.

I am sharing what God laid on my heart, the conviction, confession, and surrender. This is personal, vulnerable, and God directed me to share this with my family (who know me well) because He knew I needed to be held accountable.

I know I am strong-willed, independent, and, sometimes, ornery and stubborn. Qualities that are a double-edged blade, one side good, one side bad.

But then there is that part of me that says, *I am sixty-eight, not one, not a baby any more.* Oh, that is right, never too old to learn. Just reading about Paul. Thorn in the flesh. Wrestling with it, enduring through Gods mercy, by His grace. He persevered.

But I said to God, "I want to thrive."

He said to me, "My way."

I am afraid my attempts, my way, to improve this earthly temple, brought this sciatic flare on. This "gift" of pain, rest, and doing nothing is God telling me, *your way was wrong.* I agreed with Him that morning.

Going forward, as if I did not know this already, but apparently forgot and needed an emphatic reminder, it is "Seek ye first, the kingdom of God, and all these things shall be added unto you."

I prayed for total healing. Before that could happen, my obedience factor had to be healed first.

It is so easy to get caught up into doing what I think is good, right, worthy at any cost to obtain. But did I ask God first if He agreed with my way? No, I did not. The only point we agreed on was that this temple, my body, should be an acceptable (God defined) place for the Holy Spirit to dwell. That place should be pleasing to and God honoring. I had a mental image of what that should look like. My mental image was somewhere in its early twenties, and my brain repeated its old familiar phrase, "I can do anything if I just put my mind to it."

The lesson God was still trying to patiently teach me...acknowledge this place you are in life, accept and embrace the reality that you are 68, stop trying to be what you are not.

Why was this hard for me to do? Fear.

Of what? Death. Why? My life is hiding in Christ Jesus, salvation and eternal life are mine.

For me to live is Christ, to die is gain. (Philippians 1:21)

For God so loved the world, that He gave His only begotten Son, that whosoever believeth in Him, should not perish, but have everlasting life. (John 3:16)

Do I believe this? Emphatically, yes!

I am all for living in the moment. But back in the recesses of my mind, there was this countdown going on, and it kicked into high gear when I retired. My mom was eighty-four when she died. That means I had sixteen years left. I preferred my dad's scenario; he was ninety-four, that gave me an extra 10 years, or twenty-six years total.

But that was God's plan for their lives, not mine.

Fear is not from God; it has to go and not be welcomed back.

Death is the unknown wild card. I know it will happen, when is unknown to me, but not to God. I need to accept it, stop obsessing, remove it from my radar. Stop seeing it as a goal because it is not. It must be purged from my conscious and unconscious mind.

With the current constant daily reminders of death in the news by COVID-19, not only was this hard to do, I know in and of myself, I could not do it. This one had to go to the foot of the cross.

My prayer: "Father God, I cannot remove it, but I can surrender it to Your authority. I am in agreement with You, it needs to be gone, therefore I ask You to do what I cannot, take away and destroy it, from me right now, my fear and obsession with death. Set me free from its stronghold on my life. Finally, what I do not know how to do, but I choose now to learn how to do, with you, God, charting the course, every moment, every step, every breath. I choose to live, to the fullness, the life that You gave me, as an awesome, intentional, deliberate creation of God who is a sixty-year-old woman of God."

That morning, I receive from God the freedom to be the me He created me to be for such a time as this!

I share this personal, vulnerable experience with you, because I am pretty sure I am not the only retired child of God that has wandered down this path in the process of adjusting to life as a retired person.

Just to note, the mission is not yet accomplished; it is a work in progress. They say old habits die hard; well, it is true. But the good news is this: they can, and they do die! I keep my ears listening, my eyes open, my spirit willing and obedient. Admittedly, I have in the past eight weeks since that morning, failed. Those failures produced physical setbacks. At ten weeks out, I am doing good, but I am not 100%. I have been impatient, nothing new for me, and that is not saying it is right or ok, it is not. It is amazing that with a whole world full of struggles and problems, far worse than anything I have ever experienced, my Heavenly Father continues to demonstrate to me His patience, His grace, His mercy, His faithfulness, His healing, His renewal, His forgiveness, His restoration, and His great love!

I might add, God blessed my life with a wonderful husband and life partner in David, who is wise, caring, and loving and who allows God to use him, in my life, to instruct, correct, care for, and love me, even when I am being difficult. I cannot imagine where I might be today where it not for the love of Jesus for me and the love of David in my life. Truly, I am blessed.

I am reminded of a song from childhood, sung every Sunday at the end of the service. It goes like this:

"Praise God from Whom all blessings flow! Praise Him all creatures here below! Praise Him above ye heavenly hosts! Praise Father, Son, and Holy Ghost! Amen!"

CHAPTER 30

The Healing Power of God

Perspective: the healing power of God. We believe that God heals. We read stories in the New Testament of the miracles Jesus performed during His three-year ministry on earth. Jesus fed multitudes, turned water to wine, raised the dead, cast out demons, made the blind to see, the deaf to hear, the lame to leap, and restored health to the sick. In our hearts, we long for these miracles in our own lives. And yes, they happen in our world today, but all too often not when, where, how, in the time frame, or to whom we would choose. When they don't happen (in our desired way), how easy it is for us to become disillusioned with God. When we just want the pain gone, God wants to heal that which we don't realize, needs healing. What a blessing God's patience, with our impatience, is, as evidenced in yet another experience of the mighty power of God in our lives.

January 6, 2022. We both were feeling tired and lost our appetite, David more so than me. With David's health issues he messaged the doctor and was told to go to urgent care, which we did early in the morning. I wasn't terribly concerned about myself, but I knew if I didn't go in to be checked I wouldn't be allowed to be with David. We both tested positive for COVID. Mine was no big deal, and I was given anti-nausea med and was told I could go home. David on the other had low blood oxygen and was going to be admitted. Thus, began yet another health hurdle.

COVID is individual and everyone must make their own choices, though at times, we are denied the freedom to do so. Such was the case that morning. I was told to go home and I could not see my husband. I admit, this was a knife to my heart. Through everything I have always been at David's side. I vowed to do so the day we were married. That knee jerk response of mine kicked in big time in that moment and I expressed my feelings that not allowing me to see my husband was criminal and they should be held accountable. I was allowed to see him before I left, but was told that I could not visit him once admitted to the hospital

That is how the next path in our journey began. A path of healing, God's way, God's time, God's purpose. Physical, emotional, mental, spiritual healing.

David had pneumonia (a serious case as we were told later by the pulmonologist), exactly what kind, not sure, because everything was just called COVID. He also had some small blood clots in the lungs which much later we were told by a pulmonologist, were no big deal. His was admitted with a blood oxygen of 70 and was immediately put on oxygen. We didn't realize the time frame that morning. We both were hopeful that David would come home in a few days.

All total David spent a little over six weeks in the hospital, through January 31 in Fort Atkinson, just 15 minutes from our home, and from February 1 through February 17 at a rehab hospital in Waterford, over an hour away from our home. The first three and a half weeks I was not allowed to see David. Always the communicator, David called me multiple times every day. Hearing his voice was reassuring, but not the same as seeing and touching him. It wasn't until, because of Medicare procedures and talk about transferring to another hospital, that David said I needed to come so we could have conversations together. David also wanted our son, Austin, to come and be in the loop of things.

Things to note. David never stayed in bed, except for at night to sleep. The entire time he was in the hospital, he was up, sitting in a chair, moved about the room, and only accompanied by staff on walks. In the Fort hospital he had a respiratory team that worked with him, trying hard to get him home. Daily comment was made, "Still here? You don't look sick." David worked, as needed, from his hospital room. He stayed on top of all our household needs, and with Austin's help, taught me how to pay bills on line. He never ran a fever, felt sick, or experienced pain. Blood oxygen levels were the issue. Food in Fort was good, and they quickly realized David knew best how to manage his insulin needs. David was friendly, well liked, and despite staff shortages, his care was good. Waterford rehab facility, in comparison, left much to be desired, not in staff or care (physical therapy, once up to speed, was excellent, accelerating his progress), but in facility, furnishings, food, and working with David on insulin needs. Heart breaking for me was the lack of personal care services provided for David, receiving only three showers over the six plus weeks. God opened doors, literally, as the ban on visitation at Waterford was lifted the very day David was transferred.

What a glorious day February 17 was when I picked David up and brought him home! Praise God! He came home on oxygen and shortly after arriving oxygen tanks, tubing, and concentrator, were delivered to our home and instructions given. David was home, God gave us joy!

Physical therapy appointments were set up with a therapist David had before and was familiar with. They worked well together. PT started on March 3. Over all David lost 30 pounds, his strength, stamina, and endurance were reduced, and exertion wore him out. David pushed himself to regain strength under her watchful care and progress was realized.

Middle of April David had his first appointment with a pulmonologist in Janesville with forty years of experience. We liked him, felt confident in his care, and trusted him. A chest X-ray was done, the first one we actually saw, and he clearly explained it. It was a reality check. Before we left, he ordered smaller, portable back pack oxygen tanks that would increase David's mobility. He gave David no restrictions, told him to walk multiple times a day, listen to his own body and adjust oxygen as needed. Around the house during the day David was off oxygen, but the doctor and therapist advised using oxygen at night, but he could lower the amount and monitor. God gave us a blessing.

By May, David had done therapy off oxygen, his progress was good, he was dismissed from PT, and night oxygen was discontinued.

First week of June we went to Wisconsin Dells where Corvette Adventures is held. We both worked our part of the event with our friends. David did awesome, and it was healing for his body, mind, soul, and emotions.

Middle of June David had another appointment with the pulmonologist. Chest X-ray and pulmonary function test were done. The X-ray showed some improvement from April. The pulmonary function test gave him about 50% function rate. Doctor explained that this test is based on averages so wasn't necessarily exact. Again, the doctor told David to listen to his body, use oxygen as he felt necessary, and keep active. David had been walking, mowing lawn, doing yard work, using stair steps, taking breaks, and accomplishing, in a conscientious and responsible way, the normal daily things he was used to doing.

Early December was his last appointment the pulmonologist. An X-ray and pulmonary function test were done. The doctor was pleased with his progress. The X-ray showed improvement, and his function test showed him at 65%, which he said could continue to improve. Unless we wanted to see him, he felt no need to see David again, and we agreed. If something came up, we should contact him. When David walked out that day, I could see a huge weight lifted off him. Finally, he said, "I can just get about living life!" We praised God a lot that day!

This is the story of the health hurdle and the process of physical healing that has taken place. But there is more that God healed in our lives through this experience.

God's way, God's time, God's purpose.

Indeed, my plans are not like your plans, and my deeds are not like your deeds, for just as the sky is higher than the earth, so my deeds are superior to your deeds, and my plans are superior to your plans. The rain and snow fall from the sky and do not return, but instead water the earth and make it produce and yield crops, and provide seed for the planter and food for those who must eat. (Isaiah 55:8–10)

CHAPTER 31

The Healing Power of God

(Continued)

Perspective: the healing power of God. When we just want the pain gone, God wants to heal that which we don't realize needs healing. What a blessing God's patience, with our impatience, is. A path of healing: God's way, God's time, and God's purpose. Physical, emotional, mental, and spiritual healing.

Physical healing. As I first began praying for physical healing in David, I was ignorant of exactly what needed healing, so I prayed for the obvious—David's blood oxygen numbers to stabilize in the 90s. One morning, middle of January, God literally woke me up from sleep with the question, "Why are you settling for less than what I can give?"

This question rattled around in my head continually throughout the months of David's recovery and continues to do so even now. It's so true; we constantly settle for asking less than God can give. I've had a lot of time to consider this question. My conclusion is that we ask for less because we literally do not know the power of our great God! Even more so, we do not comprehend the reality that through the Holy Spirit in us, God's gift to us when we received

Jesus as our Lord and Savior, *we possess the power of God!* The power that raised Jesus from the dead. Resurrection power!

My daily Bible reading at the time was in Zachariah, and God gave me this verse:

> Therefore, he told me, "This is the LORD's message to Zerubbabel: 'Not by strength and not by power, but by my Spirit,' says the LORD of Heaven's Armies." (Zachariah 4:6)

I know, even after all the years I have been in a personal relationship with Jesus Christ, the literal power of God, not just for healing but in everything, is something I do not fully grasp or understand. But praise God, I'm learning! This is a personal journey. I cannot do it for you, or David, or my children. I cannot even do it for myself. Only, as I open myself to the Spirit of God in me, our teacher, can I grow in the wisdom and knowledge of the power of God I possess. And so can you!

Physical healing. I'm not settling. I ask God daily for absolute complete healing for David. This I must share. Prior to David's December appointment with the pulmonologist, I asked God that the X-ray would reveal that David's lungs were completely healed, pristine, as perfect as the day he was born. I asked God to just blow the mind of the doctor with His divine healing. To God be the glory!

This did not happen. I saw with my own eyes, shadows, though smaller, of lung scaring. His pulmonary function, though better, was not 100%. What was my response?

I won't deny, I was disappointed, but it passed quickly, and by the time we were walking to the parking lot, my heart was joyous, praising God, as was David's.

God reminded me of His constant words to me: My time, My way, and My purpose.

There is a song, "All to Jesus, I surrender, all to Him I freely give…" As it concerns the healing of David's body, this I have learned, believed, and embraced. But note, not just the healing of David's body, but "all."

Emotional, mental healing. How many times in our forty-eight years of marriage have I walked the scary path of the possibility of losing David due to his health concerns? By now you would think I had the reaction under control and the response memorized. Clearly, this was not the case.

Fear gripped my heart and squeezed so hard that at times, I could not breathe. Forced separation played a huge part in this. Over the course of COVID, we continually heard of people, families, and husbands and wives got separated, not allowed to be together at the most vulnerable time in their lives, and, yes, not even be there when death took them away. This fear gripped my heart. But I not only had fear, I had anger, I had rage, I had hatred! And I had it bad! I vowed if they tried to do this to me, I would storm the doors and battle my way in.

God knew this before it was even my reality, and God spoke to me, out loud, clearly, emphatically, the very morning David was admitted to the hospital. God said, "No." Like a slap on the face, His word came to me, sobered me, and humbled me, and I obeyed. Obedience to God is my purposely made choice since I was a child. It didn't even occur to me at this time to disobey.

The next thing God said to me that morning, and I cannot begin to tell you how many times since, and still is, God has and is saying this to me, "Carol, do you *trust me*?" By frequency alone, it is obvious how many times the enemy Satan has assaulted me, and God always countered his attack with. "Carol, do YOU TRUST ME!"

God and I had some work to do, sin to remove, house cleaning to be done, redeeming and restoration to accomplish. Did you catch my words earlier, I had fear, anger, rage, and hatred. Don't exactly sound like God things do they. Yeah, God didn't think so either. I was not ignorant of the fact and knew full well these had to be dealt with because they were literally tearing me apart, and they were as real as the nose on my face.

My cooperation with the Spirit of God in me caused this house-cleaning job to not be prolonged. I didn't engage in kicking and screaming, no knee jerk reactions. I was miserable and wanted out. It was not a wave of the wand and bam, it was gone. It was a deep dive in the scripture, verses which God generously placed before me. I listened to pastors preaching on TV, uttering prayers that exactly addressed my issues, and music of praise and worship to God Almighty.

My emotional healing was a process impacting my thoughts, my words, and my actions. You might say, "But I thought you are a Christian; you shouldn't have those issues." Truth be known, being a born-again believer in Jesus Christ doesn't automatically remove the human tendencies; it does, however, through Christ, give you the power to overcome. Satan saw my vulnerability, my love for my husband, and was ferocious and vicious in his attack on my heart, mind, and emotions.

But God's love for me is greater than anything Satan tried to hurl at me and, with His Angel Armies, fought the battle for me. When I was weak, God was strong!

God didn't waste time in bringing healing to me. Starting with those first nights home alone, God gave me sleep, rest for my body, peace for my mind, and refreshment and restoration to my soul. During the day, God gave me strength. I accomplished the removal of Christmas decorations both inside and out; cleaned the house; shoveled snow; bought dog food, groceries, and gas; handled the garbage; paid the bills; and make preparations for when David would come home. God walked beside me every time I entered what, for me, was the hostile territory of the hospital. The weeks David was in the hospital, God gave me joy, but most profoundly, God gave me *inexplicable peace.*

Spiritual healing. Fear is the demon Satan hurled at me. Lies, continual lies were his weapon. I talked to God, pouring out my heart's desire. I asked for God's help from the perspective of my finite understanding of life in that moment. I pleaded from a position of anxiety, frustration, fear, and impatience. I even had the audacity to tell God how I wanted the situation fixed. I know I'm not alone; we are all guilty of this. Then God reminded me, we are covered by the shed blood of Jesus Christ that protects us. We are healed by Jesus' stripes. There is Power, wonder working Power, in the shed Blood of Jesus Christ for all who believe, confess, and receive. My Father reminded me that His Power was *mine*! In the noise that surrounded me (lies from Satan), God urged me to "Be still, and know that I AM God!" My favorite name for God is "I AM." His Spirit in me whispered, "Carol, just let God be God!" Satan tried, but in the end, he failed miserably. Praise God!

Spiritual healing could also be defined as spiritual growth. God identifies the weak spots in our spiritual life, our walk and relationship with Jesus Christ, and speaks to us about it through the Holy Spirit in us. As we read, feed on the Word of God, listen ("Be still and know that I Am God") to God speak, we embrace, obey, and practice what we have been shown, we receive spiritual healing, and we grow in the grace and knowledge of God.

God was interested in something even more important than just healing David's body. God wanted to heal our minds, emotions, hearts and souls, and our relationships to each other and Him. God knew how it had to be done and when it had to be done, and God continues to show us His purpose for doing so.

God didn't drop it here, putting this health hurdle behind us. Nope, God still has plans for David and Carol.

We were expecting this to happen one day, even as soon as June 2023. Proactive that we are, we initiated plans and actions back before I retired in 2019. God prompted us to start preparing for that "one day." We listened and obeyed. December 28, 2022,

David received a phone advising him that his company would be shutting down and as of December 30, David would be done working. David would retire.

You would think after the year of fear Satan tried to dump on us, he would see this as another golden opportunity. If he did, we will never know. God had brought us through a greater challenge, and we were covered and protected, according to His promise to us in Psalm 91.

God is proactive too! Starting in November, Jeremiah 29:11 started popping up before us at every turn:

> "For I know what I have planned for you," says the LORD.
> "I have plans to prosper you, not to harm you. I have plans
> to give you a future filled with hope." (Jeremiah 29:11)

I didn't know exactly why, until I knew exactly why! Yes, David is officially retired. As with me, David does not have a retirement plan. It's a financial hit, but we knew it was coming and David had a plan. How long term is this plan, God knows. For now, we honestly confess, there is *no fear*! We eagerly look forward to this "next chapter," "new journey," the "future filled with hope" that God has prepared for us. Our plan is to enjoy this time God has given us. We are thankful for God's faithfulness, guidance, protection, provision, and the loving blessings He continually pours into our lives.

> Trust in the Lord with all your heart, and do not rely on your
> own understanding. Acknowledge him in all your ways,
> and he will make your paths straight. (Proverbs 3:5–6)

Life: The Teacher

Perspective—life: the teacher. Sharing one's life events and experiences as they have unfolded over the years is just part of the story. Each of us needs purpose, goals, accomplishments, growth, and some degree of success to fulfill us as a person. The strong fibers of events and experiences are woven through and help to complete the fabric of our life. They bring meaning and answers to the question, "Why am I here?"

Through the events and experiences of life, we form relationships, some lasting and many just passing as we move from one place to another. Relationships are another strong fiber adding color, texture, and patterns to our life fabric.

As individuals we have a degree of authority over the weaving process of our life fabric. When all is said and done, we must own responsibility for how our fabric turns out. Granted, there are going to be times when we have no control over the events, experiences, and relationships that cross our path. We do, however, have authority over our choices to react or respond to each situation.

Bottom line is that we are stretched and grown. What we learn and how we use it determine the breadth, depth, and scope of our growth. Do we just live life, go with the flow, and accept what is dished out, or do we grasp it, examine it, poke, prod, and move it until we thrive? The impact of life events and experiences have on us is determined by choices we make.

Before I can share some of the "stretch and grow" experiences of my life, you should know the orientation from which I come. I shared that when I was four years old, I confessed that I was a sinner and ask Jesus into my heart. At the time I had no idea the impact this decision would have on my life. Where I go from here will open the pages of my life experience as a child of God.

First, I would like to share from God's Word, the Bible, a couple of passages that have laid the foundation for my life. To do this I am going to share from two different versions, The New King James, which came first, and The Message, which broadened my understanding.

What came first was my life verse:

If it is possible, as much as it depends on you, live peaceably with all men. (Romans 12:18 NKJV)

If you've got it in you, get along with everybody. (Romans 12:18 MSG)

I do not know exactly when in my life God gave me this verse, but I believe it was somewhere in my upper teenage years to early twenties. Reflecting on this verse over the years I have found it surprising, unusual, necessary, and appropriate. There is not much to understand or explain here, but I will. God knew my life would often contradict itself, and without direction I would naturally choose the wrong side of the contradiction.

Let me explain. Remember me saying I was the child who always asked "why" when told do something. I still ask "why?" "Why" is confrontational. The first impulse is not to do or obey, it is to argue and reason. I know that I have strong tendencies to be confrontational. Here is the conflict, I hate confrontation. God knew this internal conflict would cause me a lot of anxiety, so He gave me direction on how to handle it through this verse. I cannot count the times in my life it has been my anchor. But I must be clear, I have not always made the choice to live peaceably, or to get along. I can honestly say, those were not the best decisions. Experience has taught me that God's way, was always, the right and best choice.

Over the course of my life, God expanded my life verse to my life chapter, Romans Chapter 12. I will share it in segments:

I beseech you therefore, brethren, by the mercies of God, that you present your bodies a living sacrifice, holy, acceptable to God, *which is* your reasonable service. And do not be conformed to this world, but be transformed by the renewing of your mind, that you may prove what *is* that good and acceptable and perfect will of God. (Romans 12:1–2 NKJV)

So, here's what I want you to do, God helping you: Take your everyday, ordinary life—your sleeping, eating, going-to-work, and walking-around life—and place it before God as an offering. Embracing what God does for you is the best thing you can do for him. Don't become so well-adjusted to your culture that you fit into it without even thinking. Instead, fix your attention on God. You'll be changed from the inside out. Readily recognize what he wants from you, and quickly respond to it. Unlike the culture around you, always dragging you down to its level of immaturity, God brings the best out of you, develops well-formed maturity in you. (Romans 12:1–2 MSG)

There is so much content here applied to my life but the essential action of these two verses is found in the middle of verse 2: "but be transformed by the renewing of your mind" (NKJV), "fix your attention on God" (MSG).

In many circumstances of my life, just like Peter when he took his eyes off of Jesus while walking on the water began to sink, so too, when I did not stay focused on the power, provision, and protection of God in my life, I began to sink. The verses surrounding this portion provided the when, how, and outcome for choosing to put God first in all the ordinary of daily life.

> For I say, through the grace given to me, to everyone who is among you, not to think *of himself* more highly than he ought to think, but to think soberly, as God has dealt to each one a measure of faith. (Romans 12:3 NKJV)

> I'm speaking to you out of deep gratitude for all that God has given me, and especially as I have responsibilities in relation to you. Living then, as every one of you does, in pure grace, it's important that you not misinterpret yourselves as people who are bringing this goodness to God. No, God brings it all to you. The only accurate way to understand ourselves is by what God is and by what he does for us, not by what we are and what we do for him. (Romans 12:3 MSG)

Two things here stand out, we live our lives in the pure grace God has given us. Who and what we are is the result of our measure of faith that allows God to work through us. We are warned to not think of ourselves as being more important than we are.

I went through a time when I wanted to be noticed by how I dressed, what I did, who I associated with, because I wanted to be accepted, needed, and to belong. I did it my way, and in doing so did not allow for God's grace or His plan for me.

Verses 4–8 explain how through grace and our faith, God knits us together as one body to do His will and purpose

> For as we have many members in one body, but all the members do not have the same function, so we, *being many*, are one body in Christ, and individually members of one another. Having then gifts differing according to the grace that is given to us, *let us use them:* if prophecy, *let us prophesy* in proportion to our faith; or ministry, *let us use it* in *our* ministering; he who teaches, in teaching; he who exhorts, in exhortation; he who gives, with liberality; he who leads, with diligence; he who shows mercy, with cheerfulness. (Romans 12:4–6 NKJV)

In this way we are like the various parts of a human body. Each part gets its meaning from the body as a whole, not the other way around. The body we're talking about is Christ's body of chosen people. Each of us finds our meaning and function as a part of his body. But as a chopped-off finger or cut-off toe we wouldn't amount to much, would we? So, since we find ourselves fashioned into all these excellently formed and marvelously functioning parts in Christ's body, let's just go ahead and be what we were made to be, without enviously or pridefully comparing ourselves with each other, or trying to be something we aren't.

If you preach, just preach God's Message, nothing else; if you help, just help, don't take over; if you teach, stick to your teaching; if you give encouraging guidance, be careful that you don't get bossy; if you're put in charge, don't manipulate; if you're called to give aid to people in distress, keep your eyes open and be quick to respond; if you work with the disadvantaged, don't let yourself get irritated with them or depressed by them. Keep a smile on your face. (Romans 12:4–8 MSG)

As a child of God, I am noticed, I am needed, and I belong. I am part of the Body of Christ, the Family of God. God has a purpose, a plan, and a place just for me. It is specific, intentional, and fits me perfectly. All I had to do was receive, obey, and do it, allowing God to power it, perform it, and use it for His glory. Life lived in harmony with God has many blessings.

Finally, in verses 9–21, we receive direction on how to behave and live the life God has given us. It is practical, down to earth, and useful in our everyday lives:

Let love *be* without hypocrisy. Abhor what is evil. Cling to what is good. *Be* kindly affectionate to one another with brotherly love, in honor giving preference to one another; not lagging in diligence, fervent in spirit, serving the Lord; rejoicing in hope, patient in tribulation, continuing steadfastly in prayer; distributing to the needs of the saints, given to hospitality. Bless those who persecute you; bless and do not curse. Rejoice with those who rejoice, and weep with those who weep. Be of the same mind toward one another. Do not set your mind on high things, but associate with the humble. Do not be wise in your own opinion. Repay no one evil for evil. Have regard for good things in the sight of all men. If it is possible, as much as depends on you, live peaceably with all men. Beloved, do not avenge yourselves, but *rather* give place to wrath; for it is written, "Vengeance *is* Mine, I will repay," says the Lord. Therefore "If your enemy is hungry, feed him; If he is thirsty, give him a drink; For in so doing you will heap coals of fire on his head." Do not be overcome by evil, but overcome evil with good. (Romans 12:9–21 NKJV)

Love from the center of who you are; don't fake it. Run for dear life from evil; hold on for dear life to good. Be good friends who love deeply; practice playing second fiddle.

Don't burn out; keep yourselves fueled and aflame. Be alert servants of the Master, cheerfully expectant. Don't quit in hard times; pray all the harder. Help needy Christians; be inventive in hospitality.

Bless your enemies; no cursing under your breath. Laugh with your happy friends when they're happy; share tears when they're down. Get along with each other; don't be stuck-up. Make friends with nobodies; don't be the great somebody.

Don't hit back; discover beauty in everyone. If you've got it in you, get along with everybody. Don't insist on getting even; that's not for you to do. "I'll do the judging," says God. "I'll take care of it."

Our Scriptures tell us that if you see your enemy hungry, go buy that person lunch, or if he's thirsty, get him a drink. Your generosity will surprise him with goodness. Don't let evil get the best of you; get the best of evil by doing good. (Romans 12:9–21 MSG)

Romans 12 is my life chapter. It is loaded with guidance, direction, and instruction. It is my springboard to the scriptures. When I need answers, direction, instruction, discipline, acceptance, purpose, grace, mercy, forgiveness, and love, I search the Word of God by His Spirit for the answers I need for my day-to-day life.

From this orientation, I will share how God has worked, guided, protected, and blessed me, through circumstances, events, and experiences. It will not be all inclusive, but it will reveal the areas of greatest impact where God has moved, worked, and changed my life to be the person I am today. To note: Praise God, I am still a work in progress!

Yes, I am strong-willed, independently minded, stubborn, striving perfectionist, driven by purpose, energized by accomplishment. But I am also sensitive, emotional, deeply loyal, embracing commitment, integrity, honesty and trustworthiness. I love deep, respect first, generous with trust, and embrace expectations far beyond my reach. I am flawed, I have failed, I am far from perfect. This is who I am, without God.

With God, I am still many of these things, because God made me this way. I have often wondered why. This I know, through Jesus, when I give all of who I am, back to God, He does awesome, amazing things, for His purpose and His Glory. Surrendered life is victorious life, in Jesus Christ, my Lord and Savior.

Change, Challenges, Courage

Perspective: change, challenges, courage. Remember I said God knew my life would often contradict itself, and without direction I would naturally choose the wrong side of the contradiction. Change is a contradiction in my life.

I absolutely love change. It is exciting, refreshing, challenging, exhilarating, adventurous, motivating, necessary, and something you can always count on happening in the course of life. Bring it on!

I absolutely hate change. It is scary, uncomfortable, foreign, unknown, fearful, unsafe, insecure, destructive, a predator in the dark, and something you can always count on happening in the course of life. I do not want it. Make it go away!

Try sleeping with that rolling around in your head, or imagine accomplishing something when your mind is fighting this battle. What is right? What is going to win?

Romans 12:2 tells me to be transformed by the renewing of my mind, to fix my attention on God.

One of the first verses I learned was

> Trust in the LORD with all your heart, and lean not on your own understanding; In all your ways acknowledge Him, and He shall direct your paths. (Proverbs 3:5–6 NKJV)

> Trust GOD from the bottom of your heart; don't try to figure out everything on your own. Listen for GOD's voice in everything you do, everywhere you go; he's the one who will keep you on track. (Proverbs 3:5–6 MSG)

This verse is a constant reminder to me. It echoes through my brain every time there is a choice or decision to be made. Redirecting my attention to God and trusting Him to guide me in my choices.

Having read my life story, you know there were a lot of big changes in my life, starting with Kindergarten, the first example of "I do not" want it, make it go away." One might think that these big changes often fell into this category, but that is just not the case. The hardest changes for me, in the big picture of life, have been the smaller, seemingly insignificant, but common ones. Perfume fragrance, clothing item, restaurant or store, food or familiar product, tree or structure, round-a-bouts, convenience or routine, normal, everyday things I take for granted, until they are gone, added, upgraded or replaced. I have no control over these changes, but I still must adjust, change, and accept. Once I get past my initial knee jerk rebellion, I reluctantly adjust and move on.

But then I have found there are changes, again, not terribly significant in the big picture of life, that I struggle to make and have yet to accomplish. Loosening my grip, softening my expectation, going with the flow, walking away and letting it be. Changes that reflect my OCD issues. Every weed pulled, pictures straight, clutter removed, wrinkles gone, corners squared, job completed, today. Rationally speaking, this does not make a lot of sense, but something inside demands completion with perfection. Loosening the grip and letting go takes a determined, intentional action on my part. I questioned why these changes are my greatest challenge, I still do not know.

Getting married, having children, public speaking, leadership roles, problem-solving, job change, selling the house, moving, buying a business, and retiring—these I embrace. My energy level increases, I get excited, the challenge inspires and motivates me, I feel alive! I experience anxiety moving through these changes, but it does not paralyze me, it motivates me. As the course of life moves in a different direction, I find myself drawn closer to God.

The challenge of change is to not be impulsive, or totally withdrawn. It takes courage to say yes, and it takes courage to say no. Changes impact not only the direction of my life, but others as well, and have consequences. Seeking God for direction may require patience, or quick action. The Spirit of God dwells in me and continually shines the light on the path I should take, as He leads, it is for me to trust, obey, and follow. When a challenging change is presented, and the path is not clear, the answers do not lie in what I think, feel, or the well-meaning advice of others. It is by prayerfully seeking God's direction that the path is made clear. Doors open and doors close, and there is confidence in knowing God's plan, when asking Him first, is being accomplished.

CHAPTER 34

Experiences, Emotions, Expressions

Perspective: experiences, emotions, expressions. I was at my weekly ladies' Bible study. Topics were many. I am not exactly sure what the content of conversation was when I mentioned that I gave David "The Pineapple." When asked what I meant by that, I replied, "well, it is better than giving him the finger." Their reactions ranged from laughter to surprise. My immediate thought? Oh dear, what have I done?

A feeling that I needed to explain myself got my thoughts to wandering. I soon realized there was more to this expression of what I was feeling. Like my dog when she wants attention, she nudges me until she gets it. I clearly felt God nudging me. Those wandering thoughts are from Me. There is a reason for your expressive tendencies and I want you to examine it. The beginning is always a good place to start, and so I shall.

Parts of what I will share have already been mentioned earlier, but for the purpose of clarity I will expand on some of them. There are things in our early formative years that go with us as we become adults. Emotions, feelings, personality traits, and how we express them can manifest themselves is subtle ways in our circumstances, relationships, and life experiences.

Far back as I can remember, my happy place was in the world of imagination and pretend. I was alone. I could be whatever I wanted to be, go wherever I wanted to go, and do whatever I wanted to do. It was comfortable, peaceful, fulfilling, and I loved it. Guess you could say I was a bit of a loner.

Now most young children want to play with other children, and we all know what happens then. Each one wants things to go their way. Even at a young age I did not like conflict, so to avoid it, I went along with their plan, but it was not my idea of fun. When I managed the gumption to suggest something else, I was laughed at, got strange looks, and soon found myself on the outside. That hurt, I cried, and I did not like it. I retreated to my safe place, and thus, began the formation of me "not" being a "people person," and I excelled.

I had feelings, emotions, and expression, but experiences taught me that hiding, stuffing, and silence was safe. It is a learned skill of self-protection, and brick by brick, my heart was walled in and safe from the world. I was often described as being "shy," but it was not so much shyness as it was perhaps a fear of vulnerability. My behavior of avoiding and not speaking, frustrated my parents. Transparency, even with those I should trust, at times, felt threatening and left me feeling embarrassed or ashamed.

This impacted how I viewed myself. Not just seeing myself in a mirror, but in pictures of myself, as if they had the power to reveal what I tried to hide and protect, my heart. Most pictures of me when I was young show a scowl, grouchy demeanor, or a pout. Smiles were rare, photo opts were forced, and my mother was frustrated. My defense mechanism. I did not, and still do not, like having my picture taken. There is this whole sense of vulnerability about them. When I look at myself in the mirror or a picture, they never seem to reflect the person I feel myself to be. Yet when someone tells me I have a beautiful smile, they enjoy my sense of humor, or appreciate the person I am, it is as if they caught a glimpse of my heart. Perhaps, despite my efforts, God, the revealer of all, intervenes.

Questioning, cautious, and not very trusting described my teenage years. When I hit middle school and had to walk over a mile to school instead of just across the street, I tried walking with some other girls. No matter how hard I tried to be the one walking next to someone, I consistently ended up behind them, following, excluded. At times it seemed they would even walk faster in an attempt to leave me behind. My stride was short and, carrying a load of books, I was slower. It did not take long for me to figure out that walking alone was way better, and I spent six years doing so. The few friends I did have in school all came from the country and rode the bus.

In my sophomore year, a boy showed interest in me. This had never happened before. I could not date until I was sixteen, so on my birthday in March, I had my first date. We went to a movie and it was a perfect spring evening. He held my hand, gave me a necklace, and got me home before ten. We continued dating until the end of summer when he broke it off as he was headed to college. Looking back, it totally made sense, but at the time I was devastated, struggling to let go, crying, and feeling more miserable than I ever had in my entire life.

I had opened my heart, allowed myself to feel, express, trust, and maybe love, however that is defined at the age of sixteen. Perhaps the adults were right when they described it as "infatuation." Though the hurt lessened with time, the experience was far-reaching.

It was in the fall after high school that I met and started dating a man who was five years older than me. We went to the same church, sang in the choir, shared our faith. He was sweep you off your feet good looking, and I was shocked that he showed an interest in me!

My feet barely touched the ground and I honestly thought I had met my forever love. That was not exactly God's plan. He had another purpose for this particular relationship.

Did I go into this relationship trusting, open? No. I was guarded, questioning, defensive, protective. Given his age, life experience, maturity he saw areas of my life that had potential. Though at the time I did not understand God's purpose, hindsight clearly showed that God placed him in my life to stretch and grow me, as a person, and in my personal walk with God.

It was during this time that I was exposed to other college age Christians who themselves were learning to walk confidently with God, allowing Him to lead the direction of their lives. I attended Bible studies, Sunday school classes, and other campus ministry events with Intervarsity, Campus Crusade for Life, and The Navigators. I experienced a depth of faith, growth, and spiritual maturity I had never known, and it was awesome, exhilarating, and humbling. Was I scared? Yes. But God used these relationships to encourage, lead, and stretch me to grow. By example, I was shown transparency, something that I was very guarded about.

I remember two incidents that reflect my guarded nature and lack of transparency. Comments from this man stuck with me and, oddly enough, both came after seeing a movie. We had gone to see *Love Story*, a movie packed with emotions, both happy and sad. I felt things inside as I watched the movie but did not express them. His comment afterwards was, "How can you be so void of emotion, did you not feel anything?" I assured him I did to which he replied, "You sure do not show it." Seems a small thing, but his words hurt, despite the fact that they were true.

The second incident was a double date with my sister and her fiancée to see *For Pete's Sake*. At intermission my sister and I went to the restroom. In the stall, I had laid my purse on the tank of the toilet. As I turned and was about to sit down, my purse fell into the toilet. There were other people in the restroom and I was way too embarrassed to leave that stall. When everyone had left, my sister asked me if I was ok. I assured her I was, and came out and told her what happened. We both started laughing hysterically as I proceeded to wash my purse and all its contents. The movie had started by the time we returned to our seats, still laughing. Unknown to me, someone in the movie had just died, and there I was, choking back laughter. I could tell this upset him. After the movie, walking to the car, he said could not believe my total lack of sensitivity and feeling about the death of the person in the movie. He was right, I had shown no emotion.

Late spring, he told me he was leaving for Dakar, Senegal, West Africa, for two years of short-term mission service doing accounting for the ministries of United World Missions there in Dakar. He had been working at a bank in this field of work and felt God calling him to use his skills on the mission field. I thought this was awesome until he said he did not want any ties back home and broke up with me.

Once again, I felt betrayed and hurt, except this time it seemed worse because I thought he was my forever love. I had grown in my walk of faith and relationship with God, which this time was reflected in my response to the break up. It did not hurt less, if anything more, but God assured me of a hope and a future. I was able to productively move forward in less time.

I had changed jobs and met someone new at work, and at first, we just hung out as friends, until he showed more interest. I liked the attention but was guarded. The big red flag was that spiritually we were not on the same page, and for the first time, I was expressive about that. I found transparency not only easier, but necessary, even when he had me meet his Pastor and talk about our differences. The boldness and words certainly did not come from me. God, through this opportunity He gave me, placed His thoughts in my mind and His words on my lips. It gave me the chills.

A year into this relationship, the summer of 1972, I left for two months on a mission's trip to Belgium through United World Missions. A couple that was the campus leaders for The Navigators went on this trip also, along with other college age students under their direction. Once in Belgium we joined another group from England, and together did street ministry in Waremme under the leadership of the missionaries stationed there. This was one of the most significant periods of in-depth Bible study and spiritual growth for me. Life-changing in my walk of faith.

The man I had dated, that went to Dakar, Senegal, West Africa, was in his second year there and invited me to come for a visit. Arrangements were made and I spent two weeks there. This time we were just friends, it was ok, and opened me up to receive valuable life experiences from God.

Returning home, distance grew between me and the guy from work. It was strained, but not so much for me as him. He broke things off with me, and I was disappointed that we could not be friends. But what I took away from this experience was discernment of what God approved of for me in a relationship. I also learned that the wall around my heart was being broken down by God Himself. He was teaching me that some vulnerability, and transparency was essential to my walk and growth as a child of God.

I was now comfortable to be a single person. God was my source of love, security, value, trust, and self-worth. That woman in the mirror began to look more like the woman I felt I was. I smiled, laughed, talked, was caring, concerned, and even allowed my emotions to leak out occasionally. I was still guarded and cautious, concerned about how I was perceived, but even in this, I experienced a new God-given freedom. I was not sure where life was going to take me, but I felt certain, at least for some years, I would be moving out of my parents' home and start living life as a single woman. Men were ok, fun to be with, but not as necessary to my happiness as they once had been.

New Year's Eve, 1973, God said to me, "Pray for the man you are going to marry." That came to me out of left field, but figuring this was a distant event, I said, "Ok, I can do that." I had no clue that five months from then, I would meet the love of my life, David.

What does any of this have to do with a "Pineapple"? I am glad you asked.

CHAPTER 35

Experiences, Emotions, Expressions

(Continued)

Perspective: experiences, emotions, expressions. Loner, introvert, guarded, cautious, questioning, self-protective, untrusting, quiet. These described me. When God came to live in me at the age of four, He started the work of transforming me into His likeness.

At this writing, I am seventy-one years old. Looking back on my life, well, one might say, "You have come a long way girl." I have, but I am not there yet, Praise God! He is still working on me.

God dramatically changed me from the quiet, guarded introvert, to a more social, expressive bit of an extrovert. Transparency is comfortable, expressing what I feel is acceptable. I do not like crowds, parties, big social events, close spaces. They make me anxious. I really prefer smaller groups. I can be selectively quiet, but enjoy engaging in substantial, significant, thought provoking, conversations. I do not excel at small talk. I enjoy walks by myself, reading a good book, watching a movie, and self-expression through creative endeavors. Music speaks to my soul and frees an otherwise reserved, conservative spirit.

Prayer is essential. I am a nonstop talker to God. I have times of quiet in the Throne Room of God, but more often than not, as something, someone, crosses the thought patterns of my mind, yup, I am talking to God about it. He assures me He does not grow weary or bored listening to me, and often engages me in conversation. Sometimes though He chooses silence. This used to frustrate me. I am kind of a want to know it now kind of person. God has taught, and shown me, the blessings of patience and waiting. His way truly is best, His timing is always perfect. God is good, all the time!

All of these things are part of who I have become over the course of my life, orchestrated by the guiding hand of God. He has shaped my emotions, feelings and personality traits to be more in His likeness, and He is still working in me to accomplish His purpose.

But and this is a big "but"! Beyond the times when I know God has put something on my heart, in my mind, and on my lips to say, I experience times of impulsive, explosive, self-expression. The other side of me. I know, have learned, and have disciplined myself, to not give in to these expressive impulses at inappropriate times. Occasionally they do burst forth. The shower is a good example of "bursting forth." It can be a cleansing opportunity from which I emerge feeling lighter, cleaner, with a more positive attitude.

We all have emotions, and we all express them in different ways through the experiences of our lives. God in His wisdom put the Holy Spirit in us to help us navigate the complexities of our emotional being, and help us discern the differences between what we feel, and God's will.

God taught me that transparency is a good thing. It connects me to people, creates common ground, opens doors, and facilitates communication. Relationship with others is the outcome and is

God's blessing. Transparency though, can feel vulnerable. Essential is the guidance and courage I receive from the Holy Spirit in me.

As I have "matured" age wise, I find I possess an increasing degree of expressive freedom. Where does this come from? I saw it in my godly grandmother as she got older, and in my own godly mother. Is it a thinning of our filter, boldness as a result of experience, or embracing the freedom of the Spirit of God? Despite my disciplinary efforts, I am experiencing the impulse of expression.

I have held my breath, bit my tongue, literally left the room, so as to not give in to my impulsive response, whatever it might be. During my last year of working, God gave me this wonderful, intuitive office partner. She read me like a book, and saw me in my moments of expressive suppression. At times she thought I would burst in my efforts to suppress. I also noted that as my last year of work progressed, the opportunities to express became more frequent. Why was that? Was the thought of retirement, and "that is not my problem anymore" becoming overwhelmingly attractive? Was it the sniff of freedom? My self-restraint was loosening.

This wonderful lady felt I needed an appropriate, immediate release to my frustrations. One morning I came in to work and there on my desk lay this "yellow pineapple" with sunglasses, on a green handle with a button. Press the button, it lights up and the lights spin. It is simply amazing the release that little pineapple gives to one's spirit.

Nowadays, when David, the love of my life, says something like, "Well Carol, you are getting older," I do not have to bite my lips, control my hand gestures, scowl, or even leave the room. I just give him "The Pineapple"!

Moral of my story. Transparency expressed with words and actions, under the guidance of the Holy Spirit allows God to touch the lives of those He places on the path of my life. Impulsive expressive tendencies are not removed, but serve as a reminded to me that how I express my emotions in any given experience, is a choice. My life today reflects more of the likeness of God than it did when I was four, but complete transformation will only come when I enter my heavenly home. So, for now, when I experience those moments of impulsive weakness, I have a creative alternative choice for expression, it is called "The Pineapple."

As God brought me out of hiding, He not only gave me gifts of expression, tears, laughter, hugs, and words, He gave me freedom to use them to express my heart to the world around me.

May you discover your own gifts of expression and freedom to use them, and with them, may God also give you an appropriate "Pineapple"!

CHAPTER 36

Friendships, Forgiveness, Faith

Perspective: friendships, forgiveness, faith. God gives each of us opportunities for relationships, and relationships come in all different ways, shapes, and forms. God created us for relationships.

> And the LORD God said, "*It is* not good that man should be alone; I will make him a helper comparable to him." (Genesis 2:18 NKJV)

> GOD said, "It's not good for the Man to be alone; I'll make him a helper, a companion." (Genesis 2:18 MSG)

In the creation of relationships, God not only provided for human relationships, but for us to have a relationship with Him. The perfect relationship between God and man existed in the Garden of Eden until sin entered. God created mankind with the freedom of choice, and when mankind chose to disobey God's command concerning the Tree of Knowledge of Good and Evil, listening to Satan instead, it compromised their relationship and place of perfect fellowship with God in the Garden.

If the story stopped there all would seem hopeless. Here though we see for the first time the foundation for a solid relationship, love. God loved the people He created and still wanted a relationship with them. God is holy and cannot have fellowship with sin. The only way fellowship could continue was through the sacrifice of a life, the shedding of blood, to cover the shame of sin.

Also for Adam and his wife the LORD God made tunics of skin, and clothed them. (Genesis 3:21 NKJV)

GOD made leather clothing for Adam and his wife and dressed them. (Genesis 3:21 MSG)

Here we see mankind's need for a Savior, and God already had a plan in place which we find fulfilled.

For God so loved the world that He gave His only begotten Son, that whoever believes in Him should not perish but have everlasting life. For God did not send His Son into the world to condemn the world, but that the world through Him might be saved. (John 3:16–17 NKJV)

This is how much God loved the world: He gave his Son, his one and only Son. And this is why: so that no one need be destroyed; by believing in him, anyone can have a whole and lasting life. God didn't go to all the trouble of sending his Son merely to point an accusing finger, telling the world how bad it was. He came to help, to put the world right again. (John 3:16–17 MSG)

Looking back at my life, I have had many relationships, friendships, and connections. Everything from family, church, school, work, and ministry, to casual contacts through travel, dinning, shopping, social encounters, and different interests in life. Not all of these people have been close lifelong friends, but for that moment and place in time, I was connected and God used those connections for His purpose.

Reflecting on those with whom I have crossed paths, I see the variety of ways God used them to instruct, guide, correct, discipline, humble, encourage, strengthen my weakness, and temper my strengths. I have learned to follow and have been challenged to lead. Not only did I learn the value of team work, but also how to dig deep and conquer my own impossibilities. I learned the value of change together with the acceptance of the person God created me to be. There were those who encouraged me when I was down, others demonstrated how to love the unlovely. I had opportunities to be a good listener, as well as express myself with clarity and intention. Hardest of all was conflict. Through a variety of situations God helped me have wisdom and discernment, protect my own heart, and be sensitive to others with whom disagreements were the norm. Sometimes there was anger, hurt, and a hardness in my heart and soul towards another. God showed me this was unacceptable, while leading me down a path of love, forgiveness, and reconciliation. But not all ended with reconciliation, a reality not easy to accept. Not all choices are ours to make, but prayer is always the right choice. Most importantly God showed me that He loved each and every one of them, and, like me, they are an intentional deliberate creation of His.

Prayer is another way that I connect with people. We are admonished many times in the Bible to pray for others. There are no limits on what or who we are to pray for: repentance, salvation, restoration, guidance, provision, protection, healing, victory, peace, joy, love, family, friends, rulers, leaders, enemies—the list is endless. We are told to

> Bear ye one another's burdens, and so fulfil the law of Christ. (Galatians 6:2 NKJV)

> Stoop down and reach out to those who are oppressed. Share their burdens, and so complete Christ's law. (Galatians 6:2 MSG)

> Confess *your* trespasses to one another, and pray for one another, that you may be healed. The effective, fervent prayer of a righteous man avails much. (James 5:16 NKJV)

> Make this your common practice: Confess your sins to each other and pray for each other so that you can live together whole and healed. The prayer of a person living right with God is something powerful to be reckoned with. (James 5:16 MSG)

This is just a small view of the importance God has placed on our relationships and friendships. It would seem to follow that the responsibility to nurture our relationships with each other should be a priority in our lives. God also pointed out how friendships can improve our effectiveness.

> As iron sharpens iron, so a man sharpens the countenance of his friend. (Proverbs 27:17 NKJV)

> You use steel to sharpen steel, and one friend sharpens another. (Proverbs 27:17 MSG)

This gives purpose and meaning to our relationships, as well as function and character, suggesting prudence in our choices as the impact of them is far-reaching in our life.

How do we choose our relationships, and what factors into that choice? I think it is dangerous to have a preconceived idea of what our relationships should look like. This is surely a road to disappointment and discouragement. On the other hand, there is wisdom in being intentional about our relationships. I share a quote I read from Robert McAfee Brown: "Remember that (1) where you stand will determine what you see; (2) whom you stand with will determine what you hear; (3) what you see and hear will determine what you say and how you act."

Perhaps we need to recognize that the choice is not ours alone to make. Rather, as we give each day to God to do with us as He chooses, He will bring across our path people who in that moment, need something from God. Allowing the Spirit of God to work through us, we become the facilitator of God's purposes in the world. We do an injustice to our potential and God's power to use us when we define a relationship instead of allowing God to do so. By allowing God to adjust our perspective, we will find that our life has a much greater impact on those around us than we ever imagined possible.

How do we do that? By letting go, opening our fist, palms open and upward, offering life instead of clutching it. Clutching strangles and kills, offering infuses and energizes. On this journey, we stretch and grow as we allow God to teach, instruct, and change us into the person He created us to be. Then, as we learn, we teach others by the example of our life. Whoever coined the phrase "actions speak louder than words" knew a little something about real life.

I mentioned earlier the solid foundation of relationships as demonstrated by God is love. God's love is perfect because He is perfect. Our love is not perfect because we are not perfect. Once again God gives us a pattern to follow.

> And be kind to one another, tenderhearted, forgiving one another, even as God in Christ forgave you. (Ephesians 4:32 NKJV)

> Be gentle with one another, sensitive. Forgive one another as quickly and thoroughly as God in Christ forgave you. (Ephesians 4:32 MSG)

Is forgiveness really essential? What if I just cannot forgive? To some, this is reality. This reality is not without consequences. Not being able to forgive places us in bondage that Satan surely will use against us. When we focus on our hurt, our eyes are not on God. Recognizing our need to forgive (because God tells us to) and acknowledging our inability to forgive, is a God-given opportunity to refocus our eyes and place our trust in God.

"I cannot forgive" can be also be an "I do not want to forgive." Acknowledging this demonstrates our need for God to help us do what we are not able to do. By telling God I do not want to live in this bondage, but I just cannot forgive, please help me to forgive, actually increases our trust and faith in God. Forgiveness does not erase the hurt. Forgiveness frees us to leave it behind, move on, and enjoy the fullness of life that God wants us to have.

Forgiveness in a relationship is as essential to life as the air we breathe. If you think for one moment "oh that is easy," you are so wrong. I did not mention this much in the story of my life, but like bricks and mortar, the element of forgiveness has been essential to the building of relationships over the years. Forgiveness should never be taken lightly, and should be lavishly applied, often. Forgiveness is not a "one size fits all" answer to a breach in a relationship. Though I choose not to share details, forgiveness for me has a scope, depth, breadth, of great significance in the realm of person, circumstance, and time. I have experienced great sorrow and personal pain from the withholding of forgiveness, as well as greater joy and peace in the giving and receiving of forgiveness. Just as love, forgiveness is essential to the health, robustness, and fulfilment of God's purpose in our lives, and the lives of each person we have or will cross paths with on our journey.

Just as forgiveness in a relationship with another person is essential, so too is the necessity to forgive ourselves. We have all sinned, taken a wrong turn, made a bad choice, and it has consequences that hurt ourselves, as well as others.

…for all have sinned and fall short of the glory of God. (Romans 3:23 NKJV)

Everyone has sinned. No one measures up to God's glory. (Romans 3:23 NIRV)

Praise God, it does not end there! The Good News is that Jesus died once and for all, for the sins of mankind.

For Christ also suffered once for sins, the just for the unjust, that He might bring us to God, being put to death in the flesh but made alive by the Spirit. (1 Peter 3:18 NKJV)

That's what Christ did definitively: suffered because of others' sins, the Righteous One for the unrighteous ones. He went through it all—was put to death and then made alive—to bring us to God. (1 Peter 3:18 MSG)

Remember, when God created us, He gave us the freedom of choice. Because of the sin of Adam and Eve, all people, throughout all time, past, present, and future, are born into this world as sinners. But we do not have to remain in that sinful condition. Jesus made a way for us to be saved from our sins through His death and shed blood on the cross, and his resurrection to life.

…that if you confess with your mouth the Lord Jesus and believe in your heart that God has raised Him from the dead, you will be saved. For with the heart one believes unto righteousness, and with the mouth confession is made unto salvation. For the Scripture says, "Whoever believes on Him will not be put to shame." For there is no distinction between Jew and Greek, for the same Lord over all is rich to all who call upon Him. For "whoever calls on the name of the LORD shall be saved." (Romans 9:10–13 NKJV)

Having made the choice to confess your sin and receive Jesus as the Lord of your life, we are told

"Therefore, if anyone *is* in Christ, *he is* a new creation; old things have passed away; behold, all things have become new." You have received the grace and forgiveness of Christ. Your sin, not only does God not remember it. (2 Corinthians 5:17 NKJV)

For I will be merciful to their unrighteousness, and their sins and their lawless deeds I will remember no more. (Hebrews 8:12 NKJV)

"They'll get to know me by being kindly forgiven, with the slate of their sins forever wiped clean." Your sin has been removed from you. (Hebrews 8:12 MSG)

As far as the east is from the west, so far has He removed our transgressions from us. (Psalm 103:12 NKJV)

And as far as sunrise is from sunset, he has separated us from our sins. (Psalm 103:12 MSG)

Forgiving yourself breaks the bondage of your past and sets you free! God in His mercy and love gives us second chances, fresh new starts, endless possibilities, to become all that He purposely and intentionally created us to be. There is no time frame, no expiration date, no physical, spiritual, or financial boundary, no limitation of age or imagination! Can you think of anything more wildly free than to be fresh clay in the Potter's hands?

Friendships, forgiveness, and faith are bound together in us and empowered through us when we allow the Spirit of God freedom to use us according to the Master's plan for our life.

CHAPTER 37

Gifts, Goals, Grace

Perspective: gifts, goals, grace. I have found the hardest thing for me to reconcile in being retired is my purpose, now, every day, in life. If life has no purpose, then what exactly is the point of living? I am sure this one question has haunted mankind throughout all the ages, and will continue to do so.

To answer this question for myself, I have to go to God, and He has a lot to say on the subject. The kettle is not empty, quite the opposite. It over flows with a feast, prepared by God Himself, for the total satisfaction of my heart, soul, spirit, and body. Listen to what He says:

…everyone who belongs to me, *whom I created for my glory*, whom I formed-yes, whom I made. (Isaiah 47:3 NET)

Worship the LORD *with joy. Enter his presence with joyful singing.* Acknowledge that the LORD is God. He made us and we belong to him, we are his people, the sheep of his pasture. Enter his gates with ***thanksgiving***, and his courts with *praise*. Give him *thanks. Praise his name.* (Psalm 100:2–4 NET)

However, fear the LORD and *serve him faithfully with all your heart*. Just look at the great things he has done for you! (1 Samuel 12:24 NET)

Having heard everything, I have reached this conclusion: *Fear God and keep his commandments, because this is the whole duty of man.* For God will evaluate every deed, including every secret thing, whether good or evil. (Ecclesiastes 12:13–14 NET)

So, whether you eat or drink, or whatever you do, do everything for the glory of God. (1 Corinthians 10:31 NET)

For clarity, let me just list them:

- *whom I created **for** my **glory***
- ***Worship** the LORD with joy… **Enter his presence** with joyful singing…thanksgiving… praise… thanks… **Praise** his name*
- ***Fear God** and **keep his commandments**, because this is the whole duty of man*
- *So, whether you eat or drink, or **whatever you do, do everything for the glory of God***.

Now, I have a tendency to want things spelled out clearly. Give me a list, bullet points, set goals and give me specific directions. Just tell me, who, what, where, when, and I am kind of fond of deadlines too. Now, did I not just say the kettle was not empty, but in fact was over flowing with a feast? Yes, I did. But reading the list above easily leaves me scratching my head in wonder.

I am looking for specifics, a list. Now, I know God knows those specifics because in Psalm 139:16, He talks about knowing about every one of my days before I was formed. Well, yeah, that is what

I am asking for, the details of these days I am currently experiencing. But that is just not the way God works. God never does anything half way so I can safely assume the list is complete. I let out a long sigh.

I know I expressed this early on in my first weeks of retirement. The big change from my last day of work to my first day of retirement. The great overnight transition. Here I am, eighteen months into retirement, still seeking purpose in my life. Now, to be fair, the unusual unknown must be acknowledged. Twelve of those eighteen months occurred during the year 2020 when the world was literally shut down with the COVID-19 fear. Schools went virtual, business closed and people worked from home, or they just closed. Shopping, eating out, sports, festivals, parades, markets and fairs, movie theaters, and even some trails, state and national parks, closed or operated with severe restrictions. Church activities went virtual or were suspended. We literally stayed home. Normal as I have known it was substantially missing.

I must say, I do not think I have ever been so caught up with my work around the house and yard. I found myself redoing what was done just for something to do! There was also the ten weeks that I could do next to nothing because of a serious sciatica flare. Glorious was the day the weather warmed up and I was finally able to walk outside.

Let me sum up where my search for God's purpose for my life right now is at. "…*whatever you do, do everything for the glory of God.*"

Truth be known, this is no different than it has always been for my entire life. This demands that I approach my perspective on my current life purpose from a different angle. The question is not, "What am I supposed to do?" The question is, "What am I doing with what I have?"

For this I look to God's Word:

> For by the grace given me I say to every one of you: Do not think of yourself more highly than you ought, *but rather think of yourself with sober judgment, in accordance with the faith God has distributed to each of you.* For just as each of us has one body with many members, and these members do not all have the same function, so in Christ we, though many, form one body, and each member belongs to all the others. *We have different gifts, according to the grace given to each of us.* If your gift is prophesying, then prophesy in accordance with your faith; if it is serving, then serve; if it is teaching, then teach; if it is to encourage, then give encouragement; if it is giving, then give generously; if it is to lead, do it diligently; if it is to show mercy, do it cheerfully. (Romans 12:3–8 NIV)

Reading this passage, I am reminded of what God has given me, and how He has used what He has given me, in many different ways, throughout my entire life. I remember how from my earliest years, in the midst of a task, being reminded to "do it for the glory of God."

God created me with "gifts." I was not proficient in any of them. To accomplish growth and maturity God opened doors of opportunity. Some of those opportunities were boring, smelly, dirty, and seemed like pointless drudgery. It was an effort for me to have the attitude of doing them for "the glory of God." Many were my grumblings and complaints. Today, I can look back and see the blessings.

Some of those opportunities scared me. Many were my reasonable explanations for not embracing them. But God pressed harder, having an answer for all my excuses. But He also promised He would never leave me alone. One thing only did He require, that I take the first step by faith. Today, I look back and I am so grateful for the ways God stretched and grew me. He made my impossibilities His possibilities. I am a different, better, stronger, skilled, productive person. Not because of what I accomplished on my own, but because of what God accomplished in and through me. He increased my faith, and our relationship became deeper, stronger, and more intimate. God blessed me in ways I never imagined.

Some of those opportunities were exciting, attractive, and right up my alley. I loved and embraced them from the get go. But you know, God had lessons to teach me here also. Some of the things we do just seem to come naturally. They flow in harmony with our very being, the who and what that we are. It is fun, exciting, fulfilling, and embraced with enthusiasm and confidence. The path and direction are clear, and it just flows when you step up and take the lead. Days end leaving you exhilarated on cloud nine. But these opportunities have a devasting pitfall. It is so easy to let that self-confidence become arrogance, pride, self-centeredness, demanding, controlling, lacking sensitivity, respect, and love for others. Yes, I fell into the pit. God let me, but He did not leave me. Instead, He taught me life lessons. Again, He stretched and grew me. He taught me humility and the value of being humble, being in the back ground, not the fore front. I learned how to listen, observe, encourage, let go. But I also learned how to appreciate others, their talents, gifts, and abilities. God opened my eyes to a beauty of His creation that I never would have learned by myself. God showed me that every single human being is a deliberate intentional creation of His, that He loves. God just wanted me to love them too, and there is only one way to do that. Being fully surrendered to God, allowing Him to love others, using me.

Looking back on my life I see the diversity of the many different gifts God has blessed me with, how they intertwined, and I can honestly say that I am rich with a wealth that has eternal value. I would, however, be amiss if I did not expound on the command: "…whatever you do, do everything for the glory of God."

What exactly does God mean when He says "everything"? He meant exactly that! Everything! Endless are the examples, but "endless" is not my life experience. I clearly remember moments when God brought this command to my current, conscious attention. Changing the twentieth cloth diaper filled with #2, cleaning the bathroom, dusting, pulling weeds, in positions of leadership and management, being a daughter, sister, wife, mother, employee, eating, exercise, time management, pursuing perfection, mowing the lawn, shoveling snow, picking up doggie do. I think you get the picture. When God says "everything" He literally means 24/7 from birth to death.

Perhaps that sounds like a drudgery, or a challenge to great to accomplish. Truth is, it is neither. Think of it this way: absolutely everything you do in life is an opportunity to bring *glory to God*, and that fulfills the purpose in life for which you and I were created! This dramatically changes one's perspective from "What am I supposed to do?" to "What am I doing with what I have?" Every day, we do something. The motivation behind what we do defines the purpose of everything we do in this life.

Through the gifts God has given me, and with His help, I have set and accomplished many life goals, and it has satisfied my heart, soul, spirit and body. But it is not done yet. By the Grace of Almighty God, with the days He grants me yet to live, I shall not only continue to use my gifts for the glory of God, I also look forward to seeing how God has yet to stretch and grow them, in me, for His kingdom and His glory!

CHAPTER 38

Hurt, Healing, Hope

Perspective: hurt, healing, hope. Many are the sources, circumstances, impact, and responses when hurt unexpectedly enters the stage of our lives. No one is exempt; we have all been there.

What is our attitude and approach to hurtful situations? Do we, should we, could we even have, a plan in place in anticipation and preparation for that inevitable moment. Better yet, is there a manual explaining "how to avoid hurt at all costs?"

I have some experience with different aspects of "hurt." Mine is not all inclusive, mine is simply that, mine. I am in no way an expert or authority on the subject, and like most, I floundered through each experience. It is true that through the course of my own life hurts, I formed an attitude, scenarios, and pre-planned responses, "just in case." What I have learned is that I have expended a lot of thought and energy over things that never came to pass. No matter how much I thought I had a handle on anticipated possibilities, the actual reality was not at all what I expected.

Hurt has many faces and those faces change over the course of a lifetime. Likewise, the anticipation, attempts of prevention, impact, and results of hurt have many faces which also change.

Our first experiences with hurt come in the form of "attempts of prevention." This exposure comes from our parents. Who has not heard; look both ways before you cross the street; hold my hand so you do not get lost; no running; do not touch, eat, look, go, sit, step, stand, handle, talk? Honestly, the list is endless and increases with every generation as the world around us changes. Dangers exist today that were never on the radar in the 1950s when I grew up, or even in the 1970s and 1980s when we were raising our children. I bet every grandparent has looked at their "today's generation" and said, "I am glad I am not raising my kids now!"

Being the child who always asked "why," did not always believe what I was told, insisted on experiencing life for myself, getting hurt along the way was inevitable. Even if I could remember them all, which I cannot, there just is not time and space to share. But one, I must. I remember this as vividly today as if it happened just yesterday.

It was summer. My mom was ironing on the front porch which was screened in and much cooler for the hot task. I was sitting watching her, and probably asking questions and driving her crazy. The phone rang. My mom said very specifically to me, "do not touch the iron, it is hot," and then went to answer the phone. Mom's phone conversations were never short. I sat there for the longest time staring at the ironing board, the article being ironed, and the iron. Curiosity got the best of me; I stuck my finger out and touched the iron. Amazing! Just like my mom had said, the iron was hot! I burnt the tip of my finger!

I am not one to make public all my lessons learned. I bore the pain of my burnt fingertip in silence and hiding until it was healed. Mom did not find out about this incident until I was an adult. Appropriately she asked me if I learned anything. My answer says a lot about me. I said, "Yes, I learned the iron was hot." Clearly a lesson in obedience was desired, and somewhere in the mix of things, I am sure it was.

Thing is, not always, but a good portion of my life, I am not a person who trusts, believes things just because someone said so. (I cannot tell you how many times the answer to my "why" was "because I said so." I vowed I would never say that to my children, I will explain. For the most part, I followed that rule. But I must admit, sometimes children must be told, "because I said so." The blank stare I received clearly showed my children had no idea what I was talking about. But I digress.) I have long had this need to find out and experience things for myself. Now one might say, "It was your mother, what is not to trust?" I get that, but truth be known, my relationship with my parents was frequently impacted this way. Many were the conversations between us where my parents would tell, suggest, warn me, about choices to be made, followed up with questions of but not limited to "Why did you not listen to us?" and "What were you thinking?"

I remember so well my response. It went something like, "Well, that was your experience. Does not mean it will be mine. I want to live my own life, have my own experiences, learn things myself. I am a different person than you. Maybe I will get hurt, and I accept that, but just maybe, I will not. But whatever happens, it will be mine, not yours, and I take responsibility for those consequences."

If you are a parent reading this, I am sure you can understand how much my answer can hurt someone who is just interested in doing the best for their child because they love them. Honestly, I get that, and I know in the moment I hurt my parents. However, for me, learning from my own first-hand experiences, versus being told and just doing what I am told, is truly the way I best learn life, and has served me well. Some may argue that this is immature, childish, self-centered, unwise, and just wrong. Maybe, for some, but not me. By seventh grade my parents were told they had a very independent child. Those teachers were right. But make no mistake, when I say this has served me well, I know it is because this is how God wired me. Being disrespectful to authority wasn't, and is not, my motivation. I did not further my education in college, but that is not an indicator of my thirst for knowledge, my need to know why, how, what if. The adventure of an experience into the unknown, the sense of accomplishment, the discovery of something that is new to me. These are what motivate me.

I am a different person today at seventy-one than I was at twenty, and that is the way it is supposed to be. Some of the changes in me were brought about because I was wrong, I failed, I was hurt, and yes, sometimes "they" were right. But I am also a different person because I was right, I succeeded, I was happy, fulfilled, and, because there is more than one way to, as they say, "skin a cat."

The role of hurt in my life through my choices is just one of the faces of hurt. The kind and degree of impact varied, but all contributed to who I am. The attempt to prevent hurt is a natural response that exists in all of us and presents itself in multiple ways and circumstances throughout our lives. It was clear to me early on that I walked a different path, and the difference was magnified by my sister, who, when we were young, was more like my parents. She has changed over the years and is a bit more like me, but she is also my big sister who still looks out for me.

God has created all of us uniquely different. This aspect of hurt in my life has taught me to respect the way others choose to live their lives, paths they take, consequences they experience. I have learned to be slow to judge, open to change, grant freedom, be less controlling, give grace, and appreciate the beauty of God's creations. But do not entertain for a moment the thought that I am not also guilty of doing the exact opposite because I have and more lessons have been taught and learned.

CHAPTER 39

Hurt, Healing, Hope

(Continued)

Perspective: hurt, healing, hope. As stated, many are the sources, circumstances, impact, and responses when hurt unexpectedly enters the stage of our lives. No one is exempt; we have all been there.

Preventative hurt is what I first covered; now let us investigate "unexpected" hurt. I am just going to grab some personal examples:

- Tripped over a dog, fell and cut my knee open.
- Was pushed into a plant by friend of my sister at her birthday party. Dirt everywhere on the carpet. Got spanked so hard, my dad's hand print was on my bottom side.
- A friend dropped a hoe on my head and cut it wide open.
- President Kennedy was shot and killed today.
- My beloved grandpa, its cancer, he died.
- Your parents have been in car accident.
- I am breaking up with you.
- Your son fell, cut his lip, needs stitches.
- Your husband had a stroke.

- Your dog is dying.
- Call from your daughter from college, first month, crying, she is two states away.
- Mom, I have been in an accident.
- She has filed for divorce.
- Mom died tonight at 9:30.

These are just some. There have been many, many, more unexpected hurts. You can see even from this small sampling the breadth, depth, and scope of hurt. These are all my own personal hurts, but each of them represents me in different roles, times, and circumstances of my life. One is not greater than another in that each was center stage and all-consuming at the time of its unexpected arrival at my heart's door.

I am not going to expound on the "how" of dealing with unexpected hurt. The *how* is deeply personal, and though there may be similarities on the path we take, as individuals we all must find our own way to heal. That way is what stretches, grows, shapes, and forms the person we are and the person we become. Nothing of what we experience is wasted. Each step is important, essential, and vital to the outcome, significantly impacting our future life.

There is one, and only one thing, from my experience and perspective, that I see as essential to achieving the best possible outcome from any and all hurts we may encounter in life. That one thing is a personal relationship with Jesus Christ. I cannot even begin to imagine going through any of the hurts in my life without Jesus. I know there are many people who have walked the path of hurt alone. Again, I cannot imagine the darkness they have suffered.

Though I cannot tell you how, I can encourage you with the true reality that "healing" is not only possible, but accessible and attainable. Granted, I can only share this from what I know and have experienced. Sharing my experience and knowledge alone will not help you. It is only by taking it, using it, and making it your very own, will you receive healing specific to you and your very personal needs.

My first go to, always, is Jesus. I can tell you right now, if you do not know, or have, a personal intimate relationship with Jesus, everything to follow will not make any sense to you at all. The place for healing to start, even have the remotest chance of becoming a reality for you, is Jesus.

What I love about Jesus is that He always listens. He knows how my heart hurts. He does not need me to tell Him, but He wants me, to tell Him. This conversation is essential.

I have been accused of being too wordy when I explain anything. It is true, I am. But God gave me an abundance of words because in them is healing for my soul, on so many levels. That is why when I talk to Jesus, He ever, so patiently, just listens.

By just being open, honest, wordy, in pouring out my heart, Jesus uses my own words to help me understand all the what's, why's, where's, when's, and what if's. Jesus guides me to clarity of thought, feeling, and emotion and helps me make sense of not only where I am at, but eventually, where I am headed.

There is such incredible freedom when I talk to Jesus. There is no special place, time, setting, circumstance, or preparation. Nothing and no one are closer to me, absolutely all the time, than Jesus. He is always available.

There is freedom to speak, cry, complain, yell, groan, or, yes, just scream. Jesus listens to every form of my expression, be it in soft, tender, kind voice, or raging anger. He gives me freedom to just be me.

I have talked to Jesus in a closet, my car, the shower, a bathroom, lying in bed, walking outside, in a cemetery, on an airplane, in a field with my cow, kneeling in church, in a crowd, or all alone. It does not matter because Jesus is always there, listening.

Expression is a gift from God. We all have it, and it manifests itself in many ways. I highly recommend learning what triggers your mode of expression, and learning to let Jesus guide you to appropriate restraint. Though expression is healing and helpful, it can also be harmful and destructive. God-given discernment in expression is essential.

Again, unless you have an intimate, personal relationship with Jesus, you will not understand this next thing I share. My conversations with Jesus, God, my loving Heavenly Father, are just that, conversations. Me to Him, Him to me. Yes, He speaks to me, and I hear Him. I hear words, spoken only to me. Those around me do not hear them. They are meant for me, not them. There is nothing more comforting than when my Heavenly Father says my name.

Understand this, I speak only for me. My journey with Jesus in my life is sixty-eight years long. I did not have at the age of four what I have now in my relationship with Jesus. I did not intentionally pursue any specific thing or have any preconceived idea what a walk of faith should look like or be. What I have today with my Savior is simply and only the result of my pursuit to know Jesus.

I do not, cannot, speak for anyone else's personal experience with Jesus because it is just that, for everyone, personal. What I do know, if you seek, pursue, with diligence and passion, to know Jesus Christ, and make Him Lord of your heart, mind, soul, spirit, your whole life, He will meet you in the most incredible way, designed specifically for you, by Jesus who died that you might have life. Not just life, abundant, everlasting, eternal, fulfilling, joyous life!

I have one more personal "go to" when I seek help and healing for my heart and soul. That is the Word of God—the Bible. There are so many passages of scripture that have had significant impact on my life over the years. I cannot begin to share which ones, on which occasion, for which circumstance, I do not remember them all. I just know, in the moment, when something was on center stage of my life, exactly what I needed was always provided. I do not mean to leave the impression that all I did was ask, and magically all the answers appeared. Honestly, that has never happened. What I do know is that in the journey for answers, God taught me valuable, life sustaining, lessons. He used every circumstance to stretch and grow me, challenge me, lift me up to become all that He created me to be. I am not there yet!

I do however want to share a passage of scripture that has come to the forefront of my consciousness more times than I can count. Every time, this same passage has presented itself, new, fresh, meaningful, and sufficient, yet in different ways. That is the awesome, unexplainable, power of God's Word when we open our heart and our mind to His presence and healing. The passage of scripture is Psalm 23. I share it here from *The Passion Translation*:

The Good Shepherd

23 *David's poetic praise to God*
1 The Lord is my best friend and my shepherd.
I always have more than enough.
2 He offers a resting place for me in his luxurious love.
His tracks take me to an oasis of peace, *the quiet brook of bliss.*
3 That's where he restores and revives my life.
He opens before me pathways to God's pleasure
and leads me along in his footsteps of righteousness
so that I can bring honor to his name.
4 Lord, even when your path takes me through
the valley of deepest darkness,
fear will never conquer me, for you already have!
You remain close to me and lead me through it all the way.
Your authority is my strength and my peace.
The comfort of your love takes away my fear.
I'll never be lonely, for you are near.
5 You become my delicious feast
even when my enemies dare to fight.

You anoint me with the fragrance of your Holy Spirit;
you give me all I can drink of you until my heart overflows.
⁶ So why would I fear the future?
For your goodness and love pursue me all the days of my life.
Then afterward, when my life is through,
I'll return to your glorious presence to be forever with you!

(Psalm 23:1–6 TPT)

The desired outcome of all hurt and healing is hope. Hope for better days ahead. Hope for peace, contentment, wholeness, health (physical, mental, emotional, spiritual), forgiveness, freedom, restoration, renewal, and joy.

Getting from hurt to hope is a journey. A journey takes us from one place to another. I have been on many journeys. The circumstances of each start different from the others, but similar in process. The bottom is the start where all you have to offer is your hurt, and all you have to work with is your faith, a conviction that God can and a hope that He will. Sharing from a devotional by author Max Lucado, "Healing begins when we do something. Healing begins when we reach out. Healing starts when we take a step of faith."

Now faith brings our hopes into reality and becomes the foundation needed to acquire the things we long for. It is all the evidence required to prove what is still unseen…

…And without faith living within us it would be impossible to please God. For we come to God in faith knowing that he is real and that he rewards the faith of those who passionately seek him. (Hebrews 11:1, 6 TPT)

No two journeys are alike, but all are personal and purposeful. Each serves to promote healing and growth in us, resulting in hope for us. Others may join us on this journey, but ultimately the road we travel and the paths we follow are new territory designed by Almighty God specifically to fulfill His purpose in each of our individual and personal lives. I do not know about you, but that makes me feel really special and greatly loved.

CHAPTER 40

Junk, Jewels, Joy

Perspective: junk, jewels, joy. To mimic a phrase, "one person's junk is another person's jewel." What defines junk for you? This is not something I have given a lot of thought to over the course of my life. Now it gives me pause. At first it does not seem like such a big deal, but I find myself reconsidering my initial opinion. I find myself eager to see what God has to say.

A television program that I have watched only a few times comes to my mind as I try to define "junk," *Hoarding: Buried Alive*. I also recall from my days when I worked with a team of ladies packing up people's homes for moving. Not many, but a couple of them were boarder line hoarding.

From this perspective, no way can I apply it to myself. I do not like clutter, anytime, anywhere, at all. There was a time in my life that I could not go to bed if a fork was in the sink needing to be washed, or the daily newspaper had not been properly placed in the recycle bin. I would never go away on a vacation with dirty laundry in the basket. Thankfully, over the years, I have loosened up just a tiny bit, and I still can fall asleep.

My first thought is junk is not a problem for me, but God says "not so fast." I feel a cleansing coming on, and given my tendencies, I welcome it. I am ready for the "deep dive" into my own personal junk.

> For your heart will always pursue what you value as your treasure. (Matthew 6:21 TPT)

What a powerful verse in the world of junk. When I looked at The Message version of this verse, it started at verse 19 and broadened the view. Ponder this:

> Don't hoard treasure down here where it gets eaten by moths and corroded by rust or—worse! —stolen by burglars. Stockpile treasure in heaven, where it's safe from moth and rust and burglars. It's obvious, isn't it? The place where your treasure is, is the place you will most want to be, and end up being" (Matthew 6:19–21 MSG)

A couple of things jump out at me: "what you value," "eaten by moths and corroded by rust," "place you will most want to be." These ask the questions, "what do I value," "what does not last," and "where do I most find myself?" Now it is getting personal. Feeling that cleansing!

When we first think of "junk," we think "things, stuff." But God is asking me, "What do you value?" Let me apply "value" to the filter on the scope as I look at my life. What pops up into my view now? Things like "what do I like/love," "what is my eye drawn to," "what speaks to me and says 'take me home," "what stimulates my taste buds," "what do I enjoy watching/listening to," "what do I like to read," "what do I like to do," "where do I like to go," "what is my favorite pastime," "who do I spend time with," "what do I talk about," "how do I spend my time and money," "where do my thoughts wander," "what do I like to wear?" Enough already! This has become not only very personal but an everyday, everyway, kind of personal.

Another verse is now coming to mind:

Have you forgotten that your body is now the sacred temple of the Spirit of Holiness, who lives in you? You don't belong to yourself any longer, for the gift of God, the Holy Spirit, lives inside your sanctuary. (1 Corinthians 6:19 TPT)

Or didn't you realize that your body is a sacred place, the place of the Holy Spirit? Don't you see that you cannot live however you please, squandering what God paid such a high price for?" (1 Corinthians 6:19 MSG)

Again, things jump out at me: "body is now the sacred temple of the Spirit of *Holiness*," "lives inside your sanctuary," "cannot live however you please," "squandering what God paid such a high price for." These bring questions of ownership, lordship, choices, worthiness, holiness, and sacrifice. I see a far greater significance to every single aspect of my life, touching not only the spiritual, but the physical, mental, and emotional parts of me. I find myself questioning the value I place on my own life, compared to what God, through Jesus and His Spirit place on my life. Yet, it does not stop here. Not left untouched is the potential that exists inside of me to impact this world I live in. I find myself considering just how powerlessly I have actually lived my life.

So, whether we live or die we make it our life's passion to live our lives pleasing to him. For one day we will all be openly revealed before Christ on his throne so that each of us will be duly recompensed for our actions done in life, whether good or worthless. (2 Corinthians 5:9–10 TPT)

Are you getting a different picture of "junk"? I am. I am also feeling the push to consider exactly how "passion" fits into my everyday life. Honestly, there is a pile of clutter and junk stacking up in my head and I am really feeling the need for some sorting, cleaning, and discernment.

"Junk" is a general heading or term for many sub categories listed beneath it. Let me suggest a few of those sub categories: food, clothing, jewelry, electronics, books, magazines, music, television, Internet, games, parties, motor vehicles, bikes, exercise, fitness, addictions, education, church, and travel. I doubt I have even scratched the surface, but this does give perspective.

Like most everything in one's life, junk too is a personal issue. What might be junk to one is not to another. What causes one to stumble has no effect on another. My weakness and my strengths are not yours. In suggesting possible categories for junk, one cannot conclude that all are actual junk for everyone. This necessitates an individual, personal, and self-examination. Only God has full authority over the definition of "junk" in any person's life.

I mimicked a phrase: "one person's junk is another person's jewel." Each of us are a deliberate, intentional, creation of God. We are formed in His image and God has a purpose for each of our lives. As we take inventory of our own "junk," it would be wise to include God. A verse comes to mind for direction on this task: *wisdom's guidance*.

> Trust in the Lord completely, and do not rely on your own opinions. With all your heart rely on him to guide you, and he will lead you in every decision you make. Become intimate with him in whatever you do, and he will lead you wherever you go. (Proverbs 3:5–6 TPT)

This should not only encourage but also motivate one to embrace the cleansing inventory of one's own junk. It is a personal endeavor between you and God.

One might ask, "Why should I bother, what difference can it possibly make?" So, I eat junk food, have more shoes than I really need, like nice cars, want to stay fit, and everyone needs down time, what is wrong with fishing? I expect the answer lies not so much in the possessions, actions, or choices, but in our own attitude and the power and influence we willing give to "junk" to control, distract, motivate, manipulate, and control us.

This suggests that perhaps we should pay closer attention to the things we have and choose to do. For instance, did you really intend to spend an hour and a half on Facebook when you started out just "checking" your notifications? Did you really mean to eat the whole bag of chips when you felt just a little hungry? You started out to buy just one item, but then there was this great sale and you came home with ten! How easy it is for "junk" to have subconscious control over us. Clearly, junk in and of itself is not wrong or sinful. Stop and think for a moment. Could your time and money have been spent in a better, more profitable, beneficial way? Had you eaten something different, might you feel more energetic now? You see, the choices we make every single day really do matter in the big scheme of things. Imagine what God could have done with that time, money, or nourishment. Too often we just go about our daily lives, following a learned routine, repetitive actions and choices, without giving a single thought to what or how God might have planned to use us or work through us and our resources. Are we guilty of just running to God when something unexpected crashes into our life and disrupts our routine? Is God nothing more than our go to panic button, problem solver, and mess fixer?

You see, it starts with just the most innocent bit of junk, thoughtlessly allowed into our lives. It moves right in and gets comfortable. We do not give it a second thought. But Satan does, and he is always looking for ways to drive a wedge between us and God. We become complacent, settling for so much less than what God created us for. Finding ourselves comfortable with the familiar, the routine, the everyday common place thing should actually be a big red flag waving in our face. That red flag is the call to battle. We should immediately cry out to God for help! He will be there, because God is very interested in working with us to clean the junk out of our lives. We must stop settling for less than His best. We are created in His image, and my friend, there is no room for junk.

CHAPTER 41

Junk, Jewels, Joy

(Continued)

Perspective: junk, jewels, joy. Housecleaning begun, junk exposed and hopefully the removal process succeeding. What is the next expectation? God does not remove something from our lives without replacing it. He does not leave us with a dark empty hole. Because God never does anything without a plan or a purpose; you can be sure He has one now, and it is a "jewel." Prepare to be shocked, awed, and amazed! But do not be surprised if baby steps are involved.

When junk is removed from our lives God may or may not reveal immediately how the empty junk hole should be filled. Think about how long it took for some of that junk to become an everyday thing in your life. Yes, in our world we have become accustomed to immediate compensations, answers, replacements, changes, and why would we not expect an instant replacement to fill the hole the removal of junk has left behind. We are always in a hurry; God is not. Perhaps the greatest "jewel" He wants us to acquire is the ability to wait on Him.

But those who wait for Yahweh's *grace* will experience *divine* strength. They will rise up on soaring wings and fly like eagles, run *their race* without growing weary, and walk-through *life* without giving up. (Isaiah 40:31 TPT)

I remember often being told, "good things come to those who wait." Perhaps an apt description of this phrase is "patience." But then I also was told to not pray for patience because the path to acquiring can be fraught with challenge.

For you know that when your faith is tested it stirs up power within you to endure all things. (James 1:3 TPT)

…knowing that the testing of your faith produces patience. (James 1:3 NKJV)

Faith under pressure.

Consider it a sheer gift, friends, when tests and challenges come at you from all sides. You know that under pressure, your faith-life is forced into the open and shows its true colors. So, don't try to get out of anything prematurely. Let it do its work so you become mature and well-developed, not deficient in any way. (James 1:2–4 MSG).

Though the path to obtaining can be rocky, one of God's "jewels" that He wants to create in us is patience. How much junk have we allowed into our lives because we were impatient?

Take a deep dive into God's intended "jewels" for our lives.

But what happens when we live God's way? He brings gifts into our lives, much the same way that fruit appears in an orchard—things like affection for others, exuberance about life, serenity. We develop a willingness to stick with things, a sense of compassion in the heart, and a conviction that a basic holiness permeates things and people. We find ourselves involved in loyal commitments, not needing to force our way in life, able to marshal and direct our energies wisely. (Galatians 5:22 MSG)

I like the word picture provided here for receiving the "jewels" God wants our lives to have. "Much the same way that fruit appears in an orchard." Have you ever walked in an orchard, or a vineyard, or even a garden of vegetables or flowers, when they are laden with fruit and in full flower bloom? It is visually beautiful; the fragrance can be intoxicating. You feel an uncanny sense of wealth, peace, and well-being. Should not "jewels" leave us feeling this way?

Now read this same verse from TPT:

But the fruit produced by the Holy Spirit within you is divine love in all its varied expressions: joy *that overflows*, peace *that subdues*, patience *that endures*, kindness *in action*, a life full of virtue, faith *that prevails*, gentleness *of heart*, and strength *of spirit*. Never set the law above these qualities, for they are meant to be limitless. (Galatians 5:22 TPT)

Remember the verse in Matthew 6 about storing up treasures where they cannot be eaten by moths or corroded by rust. Clearly that describes things of this earth that we might view as jewels and treasure. Actually, in God's eyes, those things are "junk."

But notice here in Galatians we are told that the fruit or "jewels" are produced by the Holy Spirit in us and is the result of "divine love." Take a closer look at "divine love" jewels:

- Joy *that overflows*
- Peace *that subdues*
- Patience *that endures*
- Kindness *in action*, a life full of virtue
- Faith *that prevails*
- Gentleness *of heart*
- Strength *of spirit*

Imagine with me for a moment the "junk" you have and want to get rid of, and have God put a "jewel" in its place in your life, and please fill in your own blank here:

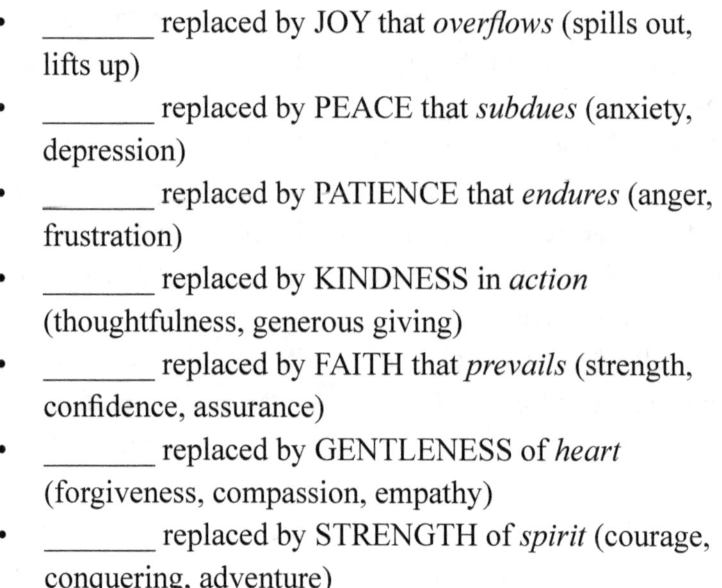

- __________ replaced by JOY that *overflows* (spills out, lifts up)
- __________ replaced by PEACE that *subdues* (anxiety, depression)
- __________ replaced by PATIENCE that *endures* (anger, frustration)
- __________ replaced by KINDNESS in *action* (thoughtfulness, generous giving)
- __________ replaced by FAITH that *prevails* (strength, confidence, assurance)
- __________ replaced by GENTLENESS of *heart* (forgiveness, compassion, empathy)
- __________ replaced by STRENGTH of *spirit* (courage, conquering, adventure)

Have you ever been in a perfect moment of experiencing something so fulfilling that you wish you could hit the "pause" button and make it last? One of those perfect moments for me is when the sun is shining, but not hot, just a comfortable warm, the sky is blue with big white fluffy clouds, there is a gentle breeze blowing, and the leaves on my Quaking Aspens flutter with a soothing sound. In that moment I feel complete. I cannot help but think that is how I could always feel when "junk" is gone and replaced by divine love, with God's "jewels."

Junk, jewels, and now joy! First, I want to make an important distinction between being happy and having joy. Certainly, we are to have happiness in our lives and to enjoy life in those moments. I say "in those moments" because happiness is the result of something great, even awesome, that has entered our lives. For each of us, moments of happiness are individually defined and have many different shapes and forms and come in through multiple circumstances and situations.

Joy is the product of Someone great and is produced "in us by The Holy Spirit," as we read in Galatians 5:22. This would suggest that true joy cannot be experienced unless Jesus dwells in us, and that would be true. It is only when we have a personal relationship with Jesus Christ that we can have real joy. But even some who do have a personal relationship with Jesus miss out on the joy God intends for us to have.

Let joy be your continual feast. (1 Thessalonians 5:16 TPT)

That is exactly what God wants for us. Sadly, we often miss out because there is just too much junk cluttering our lives.

…the Joy of the Lord is your strength. (Nehemiah 8:10 NET)

Lay claim to what God wants and desires for us to have. May we not live another day in weakness, but now, rise with new strength, and let the beauty of "God's Jewels" shine in your corner of the world, for God's glory!

CHAPTER 42

Life, Lessons, Love

Perspective: life, lessons, love. Merriam Webster says that life is "the quality that distinguishes a vital and functional being from a dead body…." Well actually that is life as a noun and that is the (1a) out of 20 plus definitions for life as a noun, and then there is life as an adjective. I am not going to go there. Suffice it to say, "life" is the act of living verses "death" or without life, dead. I would conclude then that my life began at the point of conception and will only end physically when I die, that is, my earthly life. To be clear, I do not end there. Actually, for me, my earthly death will simply mark the beginning of my "eternal life."

> For the wages of sin is death, but the gift of God is eternal life in Christ Jesus our Lord. (Romans 6:23 NIV)

For now, I can only reflect on the life I have lived thus far, because it is the only source of experience I can draw on. Clearly, everything I have touched on thus far is "my life." Like me, everyone's life tells a story. No two are alike. Everyone is different. Just think of all the people, from the creation of Adam and Eve, that have walked this earth. How many billions, trillions, or more, are the stories of each person. Think that is mind blowing? Try this, God knows every single one, up close, personal, detailed, specific, and better than any one of us knows our self. Not only that, but God intentionally and deliberately created everyone, and…God loves them all!

Our God is an *awesome God*!

The progression of our life is just a series of lessons learned. If I tried to name all the lessons I have learned, well, that is not possible, and in all probability, I would not even have remembrance of them. Like so much of life, the lessons we learn come in many ways, shapes, forms, circumstances, and experiences. But each lesson serves the purpose of teaching us something about how to not only live life but also navigate, survive, and thrive in life. They correct, direct, create, remove, improve, expand, reduce, provide, protect, launch, ground, secure, guide, build, destroy, have boundaries or not, educate, and emancipate, and I am sure serves more than this list suggests. Perhaps one could say that lessons are the blueprints of all that make us the person we know as "me."

What lessons pop out as being the significant life changers for you? I can think of a few that made significant impact on me. Never tell a lie. Breaking a trust brings regrets. Gossip destroys. Integrity matters. Truth always wins. Honesty pays valuable dividends. To have a friend, you must be a friend. Commitment is important. Forgiveness is essential. Compassion is healing. Discipline is necessary. Love covers a multitude of sins. Use wisely your time and money. Be thrifty. Waste not, want not. Kindness cost little but yields much. Judge not, for as you judge others, so too will you be judged. Treat others as you yourself would like to be treated. Honest hard work yields a well-deserved reward. Be careful how you quench your thirst. Gratitude is rewarding. Generosity brings great joy. Say "thank you" always. Love without reserve. Always do and give, your very best. Give honor and respect where honor and respect are deserved. Guard your mouth and the words you speak. Choose peace and reconciliation. As much as you can, live peaceably with others. Build bridges. Be a team player. Lend a hand where a hand is needed. Be selfless, put others first. Listen more than you talk. Strive to be understanding. Do not put others down, remember, there but for the grace of God, go I. You reap what you sow. A smile goes a long way. It is ok to express your thoughts, but do so with respect. Do not let others pull your strings, cut the strings and be the person God created you to be. Share your inner sunshine. Strength grows when you walk by faith and not by sight. Above all else, put God first in everything in your life.

Even as I share some of my "lessons learned," I find it encouraging and refreshing. We get so caught up in the stuff of life, the here and now, that we forget the road we traveled to get us here. Take some time and look back at your own learned life lessons. You will be amazed at the wealth you possess right there in all that makes you *you*. There is benefit and truth in the statement that it is not about the destination, it is about the journey, with one notable exception. The one destination that matters above all else in life is our "eternal destination." Mine is heaven with Jesus. Where is yours?

> For this is how much God loved the world—he gave his one and only, unique Son *as a gift*. So now everyone who believes in him will never perish but experience everlasting life. (John 3:16 TPT)

> A thief has only one thing in mind—he wants to steal, slaughter, and destroy. But I have come to *give you everything in abundance, more than you expect*—life in its fullness until you overflow! (John 10:10 TPT)

For the greatest love of all is a love that sacrifices all. And this great love is demonstrated when a person sacrifices his life for his friends. (John 15:13 TPT)

Jesus made that sacrifice for me, and you…and this, my friend, is "love."

CHAPTER 43

Moments, Memories, Mercy

Perspective: moments, memories, mercy. My sister shared with me how, when her children were growing up, she taught them, and herself, that the things in life that really matter, and last, are found in the many small, isolated moments in life. Snapshots to be savored, lingered over, and committed to memory. In the midst of a crazy, busy, daily changing world, I find this to be a deep cleansing inhale of fresh air and a very slow exhale.

Inhaling slow and deep relaxes your mind, lowers your blood pressure, slows your heart rate, increases your oxygen, relaxes your muscles, reduces stress and anxiety, fosters a sense of calm, and allows you to focus on the moment that surrounds you. It is suggested that taking twenty to thirty minutes a day will help you to connect, increase awareness, and quiet your mind from the demands of your busy life.

Jesus' life as He moved about doing His Father's work on earth leaves for us many examples of just how important it is to take time, slow down, and appreciate this moment we are living in our life. I cannot detail all of them, but perhaps one example will suffice to demonstrate how important the small details of our precious "moments" really are.

The story that comes to my mind is one of Martha and Mary. I think this one stands out to me because I often find both Martha and Mary arguing inside my head. As you read this short story, do you find that you have often felt this same argument going on inside of you?

As Jesus and the disciples continued on their journey, they came to a village where a woman welcomed Jesus into her home. Her name was Martha and she had a sister named Mary. Mary sat down attentively before the Master, absorbing every revelation he shared. But Martha became exasperated by finishing the numerous household chores in preparation for her guests, so she interrupted Jesus and said, "Lord, don't you think it's unfair that my sister left me to do all the work by myself? You should tell her to get up and help me." The Lord answered her, "Martha, my beloved Martha. Why are you upset and troubled, pulled away by all these many distractions? Are they really that important?" *Mary has discovered the one thing most important by choosing to sit at my feet. She is undistracted, and I won't take this privilege from her.* (Luke 10:38–42 TPT)

Things that pop right out at me. "Martha became exasperated," "numerous household chores." More times than I like to admit I have been exactly Martha in exactly the same way. How many precious moments did I allow to fly past me without noticing? Moments with my family, with David, my husband. Did he need me to listen, lend a hand, encourage, pray? Amiee and Austin as they were growing up. What small new thing did they do? Was I too busy to hear their cry, laughter, or words I did not understand? Did they achieve a milestone, need me to just listen, or show com-passion, understanding, or have patience and give praise? My parents. This one is hard as I look back now that they are both with Jesus. Is what seemed annoying then important now, but too late?

Martha was "pulled away by all these many distractions." "Are they really important?" Mary "sat down attentively before the Master, absorbing every revelation he shared" was "undistracted," "discovered the one thing most important." Honestly, reflecting on my own life hurts. The longer I linger, the more I wish I could have a do over, go back, and live it all over again. Would I change, be different, in those moments, or would I make the same mistakes all over again. Sometimes growing older is cruel. Looking back from this perspective, I find many things I would choose to do differently. Be a better daughter, sister, wife, mother, and friend. Now, as I should have then, I come to Jesus and ask forgiveness, not because I sinned, and not because what I did was unnecessary and unworthy to be done. Forgiveness because I put what was good and notable, ahead of what was best, extraordinary, eternal. Perhaps one of the gifts of a body growing older and slowing down a bit is the greater appreciation for the truly precious moments in life.

I now find myself looking at David and seeing little nuances that make him the extraordinary man he is. I draw a breath, my heart beats faster, and the love inside of me has passion I never knew possible. I marvel at God's gracious, handpicked gift to me. I am so thankful for the life God has given us together, for a love beyond what I could ever have imagined.

My children, now adults. Where has the time gone? I find myself feeling things so great and without boundaries. Their integrity, strengths, ability to overcome, and courage as they work through weaknesses and challenges. I see their knowledge, creativity, and the maturity of their many abilities. Sometimes I feel as if my heart could explode with the pride and love I have for these two precious lives God entrusted to our care. I know because I see, God has His hand on them and is always answering my prayer that they become all that He created them to be.

Often you will hear of the blessings of being a grandparent, getting to enjoy without all the day to day responsibilities. To some degree, this is true. But even as a grandparent, we bear a responsibility before God to train up, live an example, and be engaged in nurturing their life and pointing them in the direction God would have them go. What a blessing it is though to be able to just enjoy the many stages of a grandchild's life without being encumbered with all the daily things necessary to the care of them. Grandchildren are a window through which we see our own life, how it was, could, should have been, and where we are now. They are an extension of ourselves and I believe a God-given opportunity to be different, better and, in doing so, teach our own adult child as a parent.

I would encourage you to read again through the Gospels of Matthew, Mark, Luke, and John. Approach your reading with the perspective of looking for all the small but significant moments that Jesus just took the time to be present in that specific moment. To see, how in those moments, He touched specific people, specific needs, specific circumstances, and, in them, brought glory to His Father in heaven. Those many teaching moments in the life of Christ that may have seemed small, but in reality, were the most important things He wanted us to see, learn, do and obey. Open your heart and mind to receive something new and fresh that will have a life-changing impact on your everyday life.

CHAPTER 44

Moments, Memories, Mercy

(Continued)

Perspective: moments, memories, mercy. The fruit on the tree of all life's "moments" is "memories." Something, in everything, that happens in all of life, on the face of the earth, throughout all time, becomes a memory, in some way shape, or form, for someone. Memories can be shared by a whole continent, a nation, individual countries or groups of people on that continent. In today's world memories can be shared by people actually there, present, involved, as well as those who just observe through radio, television, the internet, movies, pod casts, phone calls, emails, or photographs, or many other possible ways we are not even aware of. The ways to be "present" in moments is many, but I suggest that the "moments" far outnumber not only the participants, but the ability to share "the moment."

It is interesting to note that even though a "moment" shared by many can become a memory, how that moment is remembered is as varied as the people who shared it. How many "eye witnesses" tell a different story. This clearly suggests that life's moments are deeply personal and impact each of us in different ways, leaving that lasting imprint known as a "memory."

Thinking back, how many times have we been experiencing a moment that we know, beyond a shadow of a doubt, we will remember it! Only to find years later, not only have parts and pieces changed, become something different, but in some cases only a vague sense that "Yeah, I think I remember that." Just as sure as we do forget things, will a song, sound, scent, sight, spark inside us a "memory" of something from our past. Ever wake up from a dream and think, "Wow, I forgot all about that," be it a person, place, or thing that happened. How many times have you seen someone and think, "I know that person," but have no idea why? Something familiar about them, eyes, hair, sound of voice, piece of clothing, mannerism, leaves you certain that you know this person, or someone very much like them.

Our memories are special, unique, individual, fleeting, nagging, persistent, welcomed, despised, hurtful, joyful, unforgettable, fading, and oh endless in the way they can be "recalled," or not! Memories cause conflicting responses in us. "I wish I could remember that," or equally so, "I wish I could forget that!" I am sure at one time or another in our lives each of us has had multiple encounters and experiences with the memories embedded in the little gray cells that make up our marvelous brain.

Perhaps the saddest of all aspects of memories is when through trauma, drugs, disease, illness, or old age, that part of our brain that stores all of most precious thoughts and life's moments, are lost, irretrievable, because of the deuteriation or death of brain cells. Heart breaking it is to have the one closest to you, your entire life, look at you and have no idea who you are. How frightening for the individual who has lost all memory of their own life, the places and people, leaving them so alone and frightened.

Memory is a gift from God that impacts our lives in so many incredible ways. Who but God alone could create such a diverse gift to mankind, as our memory?

I find some interesting characteristics of my memories. For instance, hurt and pain. Though I may remember a moment, event, circumstance, relationship, in which I experienced different kinds of hurt or pain, it is not the actual intensity of that hurt or pain that I recall. An example I can relate to:

Just like a woman giving birth experiences intense labor pains in delivering her baby, yet after the child is born, she quickly forgets what she went through because of the over-whelming joy of knowing that a new baby has been born into the world. (John 16:21 TPT)

Others where hurt or pain are involved include things like a broken relationship, being bullied, surgery, something valued lost or broken. I can recall numerous situations in my life where the memory of them is not pleasant, but remarkably I do no actually relive the hurt or pain. The only circumstance in which I still can feel the hurt is when it involves someone I love deeply, parent, sibling, husband, or child.

Then there are memories that involve great happiness, accomplishment, victory over an obstacle or challenge, giving, receiving, and being loved. Something deep inside me is stirred up when I recall many of those memories. Just recalling them, refreshing the memory, can bring me a sense of contentment, fulfillment, and joy, and they put a smile on my face and a warmth in my heart.

Frustrating are those things I remember in part but just cannot seem to fill in the details. What was the name of that book, who was the person that played in… I saw exactly what I want, but where did I see it? I remember that wedding but what was the bride's name? We went to this place on vacation once, and I remember it clear as day, but what was it called? I worked with that person every day for three years, now what was their name? I know I had that item, but do I still have it? Did I get rid of it? Where would I have put it? It was my favorite one!

As I said, memories have many different characteristics about them. Clear as day, vague as a thick fog, brings sadness, loss, happiest days of my life! Stop for a moment and consider all of these memories. They make up the very texture and fiber of who we as individuals are. They are singular and all mixed up with others, at the same time. Simple as a thought, complex as thousand-piece puzzle. Crystal clear and a mystery to be solved. All said and done and resurrected to enjoy again.

Some think memories are for when we are old and alone. I beg to disagree. In those memories are lessons learned, knowledge gained, experiences that stretch and grow, relationships that come and go, or grow and flourish. Do not take lightly God's gift of "memories." They are meant to be held close and cherished, and in them, you see the hand of God working in you!

Moments, memories, mercy. One of the meanings of "mercy" as a noun is "something for which to be thankful, a blessing."

Surely goodness and *mercy* shall follow me all the days of my life, and I shall dwell in the house of the LORD forever. (Psalm 23:6 EVS)

Not only are our moments and memories a gift from God, they are also an act of God's goodness, and mercy, toward us. Heartwarming is the part of the verse that says, "…shall follow me all the days of my life…."

I am left with a clear realization that nothing in my life should ever be taken for granted. These things that have, do, and continue to touch my life are not accidents, a coincidence, to be reduced to "this too shall pass." They are as deliberate and intentional as the creation of me, by Almighty God. Perhaps now is the time to just say "thank you" to our Heavenly Father. To lift our hands, heart and voice in praise for all His "goodness and mercy." To receive in this moment that which only we can receive from Him.

And the peace of God, which transcends all understanding, will guard your hearts and your minds in Christ Jesus. (Philippians 4:7 NIV)

CHAPTER 45

Purpose, Prayer, Praise, Peace

Perspective: purpose, prayer, praise, peace. This journey began the day after I retired, July 1, 2019. On that day I faced the reality that my daily purpose changed dramatically, but to what I did not know. I started to journal my days, but stopped. Then six months later, the New Year of 2020, still searching, God told me to "write." Over the past, now almost three years, I have followed this directive, with starts and stops in the course of the narrative. Things past brought forward and rewoven into new purpose in the fabric of my life.

God walked me through my life. He refreshed some of the lessons I learned along the way. Some things I thought forgotten were recalled, and others were as vivid as if they happened this morning.

Unlike many who have retired with a "plan," I did not. How many times has the question been asked, "Where do you see yourself in five years?" I have never had an answer to this question. As pro-active as I am about so much in life, always trying to get a jump on things, being well prepared, efficient, I have not been as it concerns my own personal "tomorrows." To be clear, this does not leave me puzzled, scratching my head, wondering why. I know why. My life, by choice, has been a daily walk of faith. Following the path God prepared for me. Waking in the morning not knowing by days end what the day would bring but assured that God always knew and was in control.

Many of those days were just as God planned them, some were not. I made wrong choices, did not listen to God or follow the path He put before me. But none of my days were wasted. God's purpose for my life was always served.

What I have come to know, through this process of searching for purpose, is that from God's perspective, my purpose, His reason for creating me, has never changed.

Whether you eat or drink, live your life in a way that glorifies and honors God. (1 Corinthians 10:31 TPT)

One of my favorite passages of scripture is found in the first two verses of my life chapter, Romans 12, and I love the way it is laid out in The Message. I share them again:

So, here's what I want you to do, God helping you: Take your everyday, ordinary life—your sleeping, eating, going-to-work, and walking-around life—and place it before God as an offering. Embracing what God does for you is the best thing you can do for him. Don't become so well-adjusted to your culture that you fit into it without even thinking. Instead, fix your attention on God. You'll be changed from the inside out. Readily recognize what he wants from you, and quickly respond to it. Unlike the culture around you, always dragging you down to its level of immaturity, God brings the best out of you, develops well-formed maturity in you. (Romans 12:1–2 MSG)

My purpose in life is not to be a daughter, a sister, a friend, a wife, a mother, a business owner, a team player, an employee, an administrative assistant, a department head, or any one of the many hats I have worn throughout the course of my life. My purpose, in all of things I have done my entire life, was to do each one in a way that brings honor and glory to God.

Retirement does not change the purpose of my life for which God deliberately and intentionally created me. Period!

This reality infuses me with energy, excitement, enthusiasm, commitment, joy, and hope! My purpose did not end the day I retired; it simply changed location. One door closed, but I cannot even begin to count the number of doors, that remain open. The only restrictions I will experience, will be placed there by me, not God. I have nothing to fear, no reason to be anxious. I simply must do what I have always done, open my arms, my hands, my heart, and receive God's best blessings!

Paul, in writing to the Thessalonians, encouraged them to keep on going with what God had given them to do right up until Jesus returns. No retirement here. His prayer for them was that God would continue to not only make them fit for the work they were called to do but also to allow God to energize their ideas and acts of faith and in so doing honor God. Grace, in and through it, freely given.

Because we know that this extraordinary day is just ahead, we pray for you all the time—*pray that our God will make you fit for what he's called you to be, pray that he'll fill your good ideas and acts of faith with his own energy so that it all amounts to something.* If your life honors the name of Jesus, he will honor you. *Grace is behind and through all of this, our God giving himself freely, the Master, Jesus Christ, giving himself freely.* (2 Thessalonians 1:11–12 MSG)

Though I have given consideration to my limitations of age, energy, and physical dexterity, I realize that God gives me what

I need to complete His purpose and will for my life. Extravagant grace is freely given, and mine just for the asking.

Prayer is the key, but faith unlocks the door. I heard this repeated often from the time I was a teenager, and as I grew in my walk with Jesus, it became and was confirmed over and over, to be true. Prayer is as essential to everything in our spiritual life, as breathing air is to our physical life.

Great is the similarity of prayer and breathing. Most notable, we do not think about each breathe that we take. Though sometimes it might be intentional; for 99.9% of our life, it just happens. Over the ages man has tried to make prayer something it is not. Brought to mind are the Pharisees, obsessed with how, where, when, what to wear, and who was watching. God called them hypocrites. Books have been written on prayer, instructions given, process to follow, breaking prayer down into segments and procedures. The "must do's" if you want your prayers to be heard and answered. I do not agree. As with breathing, so too is praying.

Are there any believers in your fellowship suffering great hardship and distress? Encourage them to pray! Are there happy, cheerful ones among you? Encourage them to sing out their praises! Are there any sick among you? Then ask the elders of the church to come and pray over the sick and anoint them with oil in the name of our Lord. And the prayer of faith will heal the sick and the Lord will raise them up, and if they have committed sins they will be forgiven. Confess and acknowledge how you have offended one another and then pray for one another to be instantly healed, for tremendous power is released through the passionate, heartfelt prayer of a godly believer! (James 5:13–16 TPT)

There is a lot of content here, but let me pull out what stands out to me regarding prayer. "Encourage them to pray," "pray over the sick…in the name of our Lord," "prayer of faith will heal," "pray for one another," and "tremendous power is released through the passionate, heartfelt prayer of a godly believer!" Now I realize that this passage of scripture seems to be specific in the area of healing, but that actually validates how essential prayer in our lives is. What prompts most people to turn to prayer? Suffering, hardship, distress, illness, and things from which we seek relief and healing. In the world of prayer, these are big ticket items.

But let me go one step further. God instructs us to not only be intentional in our prayer but also to make prayer our living breathing, way of life.

Make your life a prayer. (1 Thessalonians 5:17 TPT)

Stop for a moment, and let that sink deep into your very being. Consider exactly what that literally means.

Breathing is so personal. Breathing is our physical life; when we stop breathing, we stop living.

Prayer is so personal. Prayer is our spiritual life; when we stop praying, we stop living. Our prayers come directly from our heart and are grounded in our personal relationship with Jesus. As breathing is life, prayer is life.

Because prayer is so personal, between ourselves and God, I cannot tell you what is right for you or how it should be. I can only share the role prayer has in my own life. Prayer, for me, is whispers from my heart, words spoken with my voice, and thoughts formed in my mind. Prayer is how I talk to God, and how God talks to me. There is no sanctioned spot where I must be in order to talk to God. Anywhere, anytime, anyway, I am free to reach out to my Abba Father, and I know He hears me, because He answers me. These words do not do justice to the vital importance of prayer, talking to God, in my life. I just know, I cannot exist without prayer, and nothing, no one, can ever take it away from me.

I talk to God about everything. Was God always my first "go to"? No. Do I even now still try and work things out by myself first, ashamedly, yes. At times I have wondered if God gets sick of listening to me, you know, being a "wordy" person. He does not, He made me wordy and fully expects me to be wordy. Is there anything that is too "unholy" to talk to God about? I assure you, there is not. Is there anything, circumstance, situation, or place, that is unacceptable to talk to God. Again, no.

I come back to this passage from Proverbs. It is the grounding foundation to living life, each moment, each breathe, always, forever.

> Trust in the Lord completely, and do not rely on your own opinions. With all your heart rely on him to guide you, and he will lead you in every decision you make. Become intimate with him in whatever you do, and he will lead you wherever you go. (Proverbs 3:5–6 TPT)

Praise is the response of my heart for all that God has done for me! Praise is an action, expression of thanksgiving, an offering, a sacrifice, from my heart to a most Holy God. We all are instructed to offer praise at all times, in all circumstances.

> Through him then let us continually offer up a sacrifice of praise to God, that is, the fruit of our lips, acknowledging his name. (Hebrews 13:15 NET)

Praise is not forced, is beyond choice, has no boundaries, and is limitless, expressive, personal, corporate, life giving, spirit lifting, soul filling, and all consuming. Our expression of praise is an outward demonstration of our inner gratitude and love for all our

Savior, Jesus Christ, has done for us, to the one true Almighty God of Angel Armies! Hallelujah!

What can I expect if I seek God first in all things, obey what He tells me to do, walk by faith, not by sight, trust God completely, and offer a sacrifice of praise?

I am not guessing when I tell you that I know what it is to "be loved," and to "have peace." This is not something I wonder about or question when it will happen. It is a reality that I have experienced. I suspect that now I know love and peace only in part, but I am assured that one day I will experience it complete and full, and it will be something that I cannot even begin to imagine now, just as the words in the song by Mercy Me, "I Can Only Imagine," suggest. They are like a peek through a small hole in the fence, allowing me to see in part, leaving me longing to know in full, what is on the other side. Meantime, my Heavenly Father points me forward. Instructs me to walk in His ways. Live in a way that brings Honor and Glory to His Name. In doing this I am assured that my life will have direction, meaning, purpose, and fulfilment.

Words of peace to encourage us in our day to day lives are found in the book of John, spoken by Jesus. Highlighted are words to ponder, embrace, absorb, and be allowed to empower you through the Spirit of God living in you:

Jesus replied, "*Loving me empowers you to obey my word. And my Father will love you so deeply that we will come to you and make you our dwelling place.* But those who do not love me will not obey my words. The Father did not send me to speak my own revelation, but the words of my Father. I am telling you this while I am still with you. But when *the Father sends the Spirit of Holiness, the One like me who sets you free*, he will *teach you all things in my name*. And he will *inspire you to remember every word that I have told you. I leave the gift of peace with you—my peace*. Not the kind of fragile peace given by the world, but *my perfect peace. Don't yield to fear or be troubled in your hearts—instead, be courageous!*" (John 14:23–27 TPT)

Not only words of peace to encourage us, but words of God's love to empower us to live as confident conquerors every day.

Yet even *in the midst of all these things, we triumph over them all, for God has made us to be more than conquerors*, and his demonstrated love is our glorious victory over everything! So now I *live with the confidence that there is nothing in the universe with the power to separate us from God's love. I'm convinced that his love will triumph over death, life's troubles, fallen angels, or dark rulers in the heavens. There is nothing in our present or future circumstances that can weaken his love. There is no power above us or beneath us— no power that could ever be found in the universe that can distance us from God's passionate love*, which is lavished upon us through our Lord Jesus, the Anointed One! (Romans 8:37–39 TPT)

Mine is the life that God created me to have. Had I chosen to not surrender my will to that of my Heavenly Father I am sure beyond doubt that who and what I am today would be, well, in comparison, unrecognizable. There was a time in life that I felt cheated out of the awesome, life-changing experience of being saved by Jesus out of a life of experienced sin. How different my story would be! From my perspective today I am grateful that Jesus captured my heart at the age of four. As we live our lives, have experiences, we catch glimpses of who we could have been, how we might have acted, choices we that might have made, had it not been for the grace of God. I have had those glimpses; they are not good. God is His wisdom, love, mercy, and grace that saved me from me.

I look forward to the sunrise of the days, months, and years, I have left of this earth. In them I know God has a plan, direction, and purpose. I know too that in every moment God, as Lord of my life, will be in charge, in control, and nothing thrown at me will harm me, because I live in the power of Jesus, who lives, dwells, and reigns in my life. I made, and will continue to make, the choice of obedience as "all to Jesus, I surrender." *Even so, "Come Lord Jesus!"*

CHAPTER 46

God's Promise:
Safe and Secure

Perspective: safe and secure. We all want a degree of safety and security. Knowing, claiming, and living in the power of the Promises of God will give us exactly what we need and desire. I leave you with the promise of Psalm 91 (MSG). Embrace it as part of your everyday life.

God's blessings!

Safe and Secure

1–13 You who sit down in the High God's presence,
spend the night in Shaddai's shadow,
Say this: "GOD, you're my refuge.
I trust in you and I'm safe!"
That's right—he rescues you from hidden traps,
shields you from deadly hazards.
His huge outstretched arms protect you—under them you're
perfectly safe; his arms fend off all harm.

Fear nothing—not wild wolves in the night,
not flying arrows in the day,
not disease that prowls through the darkness,
not disaster that erupts at high noon.
Even though others succumb all around,
drop like flies right and left, no harm will even graze you.
You'll stand untouched, watch it all from a distance,
watch the wicked turn into corpses.
Yes, because GOD's your refuge,
the High God your very own home,
Evil can't get close to you; harm can't get through the door.
He ordered his angels to guard you wherever you go.
If you stumble, they'll catch you;
their job is to keep you from falling.
You'll walk unharmed among lions and snakes,
and kick young lions and serpents from the path.

14-16 "If you'll hold on to me for dear life," says GOD,
"I'll get you out of any trouble.
I'll give you the best of care if you'll only
get to know and trust me.
Call me and I'll answer, be at your side in bad times;
I'll rescue you, then throw you a party.
I'll give you a long life, give you a long drink of salvation!"